Devotions
BY DEAD PEOPLE

secrets of life from beyond the grave

Lynn Lusby Pratt

EMPOWERE
Stand
Cin

Scripture quotations marked NIV are taken from the HOLY BIBLE, NEW INTERNATIONAL VERSION®. NIV®. Copyright © 1973, 1978, 1984 by International Bible Society. Used by permission of Zondervan. All rights reserved.

Scripture quotations marked NLT are taken from the Holy Bible, *New Living Translation*, copyright © 1996. Used by permission of Tyndale House Publishers, Inc., Wheaton, Illinois 60189. All rights reserved.

Scripture quotations marked ICB are taken from the *International Children's Bible® New Century Version®*. Copyright © 1986, 1988, 1999 by Tommy Nelson™, a division of Thomas Nelson, Inc., Nashville, Tennessee 37214. Used by permission.

Scripture quotations marked KJV are taken from the *King James Version*.

Cover and inside design by Ahaa! Design
Cover and inside photos by David Strasser
Edited by Dale Reeves

Library of Congress Cataloging-in-Publication Data:
Pratt, Lynn Lusby.
    Devotions by dead people : secrets of life from beyond the grave /
Lynn Lusby Pratt.– 1st American pbk. ed.
        p. cm.
    ISBN 0-7847-1528-9 (pbk.)
1. Young adults–Prayer-books and devotions–English. 2. Death–Biblical teaching. I. Title.
BV4850.P728 2004
242'.63–dc22

                                                            2004001924

© 2004 by Lynn Lusby Pratt
All rights reserved.
EMPOWERED® Youth Products is a trademark of Standard Publishing.
Printed in the United States of America.

Standard Publishing, Cincinnati, Ohio.
A Division of Standex International Corporation.

11   10   09   08   07   06   05   04
7   6   5   4   3

ISBN: 0-7847-1528-9

Dedication

in memory
Mark Pratt
1950—2000

Last words:
"Love. God. More."

Contents

Introduction

Ever thought about what will be on your tombstone? Check out this epitaph:

> Here lies John Bun;
> He was killed by a gun.
> His name was not Bun, but Wood.
> But Wood would not rhyme with gun, and Bun would.

Those words tell us quite a bit about John. Poor John died a violent death. But his life must have been kind of fun, since his family or friends composed that funny epitaph to remember him with a smile.

We have a fascination with death—whether it's our own or someone else's. We like to talk about all the related topics: things like Heaven and Hell, ghosts, murder, angels, zombies and the afterlife. And just look at the lineup of movies in the TV program for a given week: *Death on the Nile, Dead Man, Die Hard, Dracula: Dead and Loving It, Deadly Betrayal, Dead Presidents* . . . When it comes to death, we just can't seem to get enough.

Perhaps, in our obsession with death, we're really searching for meaning in life. In this book you'll meet real live dead people. You'll walk through ancient graveyards, as it were, and read what might have been their epitaphs. You'll discover their causes of death and hear their last words. Other stats, quotes and eerie Bible stories will unveil more secrets.

If you read the chapters in order, you'll get an overview of Bible history. The entries generally follow the biblical narrative from Genesis to Revelation—with one exception: the best has been moved to last. If you prefer, go to the topical index in the back and choose something of interest. Or just open the book anywhere to resurrect the truth of a long-dead character. What you learn about their deaths may change your life.

—LLP

✝ I Hear Dead People

Here Lies
Abel, the world's first murder victim

THE BODY

Abel died on page four. *How can he be important enough to mention, I wondered, if he doesn't even appear in the rest of the book?*

Then I remembered Rebecca.

She's the main character in the gothic novel *Rebecca,* but she doesn't appear in the book at all . . . at least, not bodily. She's already dead, but Rebecca de Winter still influences the residents of the mansion: Mr. de Winter has been moody and restless since her death; the new bride is in torment trying to fill Rebecca's shoes. And then there's Mrs. Danvers, the creepy housekeeper, who is haunted by Rebecca's absence. "Sometimes," she says, "when I walk along the corridor here I fancy I hear her just behind me. That quick, light footstep. I could

cause of death
Murdered by his brother Cain (Genesis 4:8).

last words
No words of Abel are recorded in Scripture.

life line ⎯〰〰〰

"Set the standard for excellence early."

—Bob Russell, minister of the 12,000 member Southeast Christian Church, Louisville, Kentucky

WORDS TO LIVE BY

"Abel brought the best."

Genesis 4:4, ICB

not mistake it anywhere."

Rebecca lives on.

Abel died on page four of a 1300-page Bible without leaving us a record of any words he spoke. But page 1262 (which takes place maybe 3,000 years later) says Abel is still speaking! And we're reading about Abel 2,000 more years after that.

Abel lives on.

God thought Abel was worth mentioning in the Bible. Abel brought the best of his sheep as an offering to God. It was generous. It was excellent. His brother Cain brought an offering too, something from the soil. Maybe it was some fruit, some vegetables or some grain. But his heart wasn't in it—it was just some old offering. Abel's offering made Cain look bad. So Cain murdered Abel—"because his own actions were evil and his brother's were righteous" (1 John 3:12, NIV).

Abel's death doesn't seem fair. Abel was the good guy. But, in case you haven't noticed, sometimes the bad guys kill the good guys. In the end, how Abel lived is more important than how

EPITAPH

Tranquil & silent here lies Dill,

What gifts he had he managed well.

He did his best to merit fame

And left behind him a good name.

Remember Dill and do the same.

—in Vermont, died 1804

8

HEART-STOPPER

Mahatma Ghandi was the beloved leader of India who promoted peace. After he was gunned down by an assassin, someone said, "Now we know how dangerous it is to be good."

Abel died. And Abel lived excellently.

Do you have a test coming up? Do your best. Are you cleaning your room tomorrow? Do your best. Do you have a part in the school play? Do your best. Bringing an offering to God in worship? Do your best.

Whatever you do, give your best to God.

Abel is still speaking, by his actions, thousands of years after his death: "Do your best. Do your best."

Can you hear him? Listen to Abel. And live on.

 midnight tale

They, being dead, still earn money! The August 2003 *Reader's Digest* listed the dead celebrities who are bringing in the most money:

No. 1—Elvis (the king of rock and roll)

No. 2—Charles Schulz (creator of the *Peanuts* comic strip)

No. 3—John Lennon (of The Beatles)

No. 4—Dale Earnhardt (race car driver)

in memory of
Abel

"By faith Abel offered God a better sacrifice than Cain did. . . .
And by faith he still speaks, even though he is dead."

Hebrews 11:4, NIV

✝HE UⲚDEAD

Here Lies
Enoch, who walked with God

✝HE BODY

He vanished one day in 1975. Jimmy Hoffa was the powerful boss of the Teamsters labor union. Most people believed that he was the victim of a mob hit. A short time after his disappearance, Jimmy Hoffa was presumed dead. In 1982 he was declared legally dead, even though his body had not been found. His story was a hot topic for years (and still is!). When my sister's family was moving, they pulled the washer and dryer away from the wall. There was such a huge pile of dust back there, someone shouted, "Hey, I think we've found Jimmy Hoffa!"

Enoch vanished one day before the year 2000 B.C. He was probably presumed dead, then declared legally dead. How

cause of death
He didn't die. But at age 365 . . .

last words
The only words of Enoch in the Bible appear long after he lived. Jude quoted words of Enoch that were in a book that is not part of our Scriptures: "Look, the Lord is coming with thousands and thousands of his holy angels. . . . He is coming to judge everyone and to punish all who are against God" (Jude 14, 15, ICB).

WORDS TO LIVE BY

*"Teach me your way,
El LORD, and I will
walk in your truth."*

Psalm 86:11, NIV

long did his family keep looking for him? ("Hey, look at all the dust under this bed. I think we've found Enoch!") Was Enoch the victim of a mob hit?

Genesis 5:24 says Enoch "was no more" (NIV). Hebrews 11:5 spells it out clearly: "Enoch was taken from this life, so that he did not experience death; he could not be found, because God had taken him away" (NIV).

Whoa. What made Enoch so special that God let him skip dying?

"Enoch walked with God" (Genesis 5:24, NIV).

What does that mean—to walk with God?

God says that his Word is "a light for my path" (Psalm 119:105, NIV). When we do what he says in his Word, we are walking with him. His commands shine a light on our paths and whisper, "Here, this is the right way. Walk with me."

Being in the dark, being a little scared, is fun—as long as you know where the light switch is. Some people don't know where the light switch is. Spiritual things are hot topics today. But some ideas that are "spiritual" may not be on target. We have to stay on track. Proverbs 6:22 shows us

EPITAPH

Here lies a man that was
  KNOTT born,
His father was KNOTT
  before him,
He lived KNOTT, and did
  KNOTT die,
Yet underneath this stone
  doth lie.

—in Sheffield, England

exactly how God's commands keep us walking in the light with God:

"When you walk, they will guide you;
When you sleep, they will watch over you;
When you awake, they will speak to you" (NIV).

When Jude quoted Enoch's last words, Jude was trying to make a point about people who don't believe in God, who don't walk with God. Jude said those people were headed for "blackest darkness" (Jude 13). They didn't know where the light switch was. But Jesus said that whoever followed in God's way would "never walk in darkness, but will have the light of life" (John 8:12, NIV).

When we walk with God we'll be able to see the way to really live.

We don't know any details of Enoch's life—what he looked like or what his job was. All we know about Enoch is that Enoch walked with God.

That says it all.

Elijah is the only other Bible character who did not experience death (2 Kings 2). But one other entire group of people will not experience death, according to the Bible. When Jesus comes back, "the dead in Christ will rise first. After that, we who are still alive . . . will be caught up together with them in the clouds to meet the Lord in the air. And so we will be with the Lord forever" (1 Thessalonians 4:16, 17, NIV).

in memory of
Enoch

"Let us walk in the light of the LORD."
Isaiah 2:5, NIV

✝ When Time Runs Out

Here Lies
Methuselah, the oldest man who ever lived

THE BODY

I once saw a silly watch. The numbers, instead of being neatly spaced around the edges of the circle, were all jumbled together in the 7:00 area—as if they'd come unglued and slipped down. In the middle of the watch face was one word: *Whatever!* I guess you give a watch like that to someone who is always late or has a very casual view of time.

Methuselah could afford to have a casual view of time. He had all the time in the world. He lived to be 969 years old.

That is not going to happen to you.

All things being equal, you can expect to live to be 70 or 80 years old. But all things are *not* equal. People in

cause of death
At age 969, what else? Old age! (Genesis 5:27).

last words
There are no recorded words of Methuselah in Scripture. But he had to have been spunky. Maybe as everyone gathered around his deathbed, he moaned, "Aw, guys, I was just getting started."

DEATH SENTENCE
We assume Methuselah was one of the good guys. He was the son of Enoch and the grandfather of Noah. Good family.

Make "the most of every opportunity."
Ephesians 5:15, NIV

their 30s die. Toddlers die. Teenagers die.

In some cases, teenagers are very aware of time. A year is very important if you don't make the cut in tryouts and have to wait a whole year for the next chance. A month is important if your boyfriend is out of town that long. One minute is important when you're holding your boarding pass—and watching the plane taxi away. Even a fraction of a second is important if you happen to be a sprinter.

But you may not think much about the daily *tick-tock, tick-tock.* You may not be very concerned about how you spend an average day.

Guess what? Other people are after your time. There are over 24,000 movie rental stores urging you to spend time watching one of their movies. There are over 700 amusement parks saying, "Spend the day with us." There are over 50,000 commercial sports events wanting you to come and spend several hours cheering the team.

It's interesting that we use the word *spend* when referring to time. We spend money. We spend time. The difference is that we also have the

SIX-FEET-DEEP THOUGHT
"All time belongs to you if you belong to Christ."
—E. Stanley Jones

option of saving money. We can't save time. We talk about saving time, but we really can't do that. Snap your fingers. That second is gone. And that one. And that one. You can't save the seconds. They're gone and they're not coming back. All you can do with time is spend it.

Methuselah was really just like you as far as time is concerned. He lived to be 969, but he didn't know how long he was going to live. Every morning he only had today. You don't know how long you will live. Every morning you only have today.

What would happen if you began every morning with "God thoughts" about today?

"Today we know that the LORD is with us" (Joshua 22:31, NIV).

"Today listen to what [God] says" (Psalm 95:7, ICB).

"Today I will give the carcasses . . ." (OK, maybe we don't need that one, but it's 1 Samuel 17:46, NIV).

"O LORD, . . . give me success today" (Genesis 24:12, NIV).

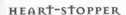

HEART-STOPPER

"I thank the Lord today!" (1 Kings 5:7, ICB).

God will give us important things to do if we give our "todays" to him. Let's get our numbers glued back in place. Let's erase the word *Whatever!* from our faces.

It's time.

in memory of
Methuselah

"The time has come for my departure."
2 Timothy 4:6, NIV

Quoth the Raven, "Nevermore."

Here Lies
Noah, survivor of the great flood

THE BODY

Noah had never seen an ark (a ship the size of an ocean liner).

Noah had never seen rain. There was no such thing . . . yet.

Noah had probably never seen a flood.

When God said, "Noah, build an ark. The rain I'm sending will cause a world-wide flood," Noah must have replied, "Huh?"

But he believed God and got busy. He knew God was true to his word.

How long it must have taken Noah to construct the ark! And it would have *felt* even *longer*—Genesis 6:11 says the other people were anti-God and violent. They must've hassled him. But Noah held on to God and

cause of death
Unknown, at age 950 (Genesis 9:29).

last words
Oddly, Noah's last recorded words are a curse on the Canaanites, who were the descendants of his son Ham. He blessed the descendants of his other two sons, Shem and Japheth, but predicted Ham's descendants would be their slaves (Genesis 9:25-27).

WORDS TO LIVE BY

*"Has [God] ever spo-
ken and failed to
act? Has he ever
promised and not
carried it through?"*

Numbers 23:19, NLT

Never!

kept working.

And then . . .

H$_2$Oh!

Forty days and nights of rain. Eight people safe in the ark, and—some teachers believe—nearly one billion human bodies starting to float. (That's a pleasant thought.)

Noah's family was inside the ark for more than a year—a year Noah must have felt would never end. But Noah hung on. Noah had seen God keep his promise to destroy the earth. He believed God would keep his promise to save Noah's family. No doubt he'd learned that God always keeps his promises. After all, Noah was already 600 years old. He and God had spent a *lot* of time together.

Finally, Noah released a raven to scope out the conditions outside. He also sent a dove—but the dove came back. There was still no nice place for nesting. Later, a dove was sent out again, and it returned with a fresh olive tree leaf—things were looking up. Still later a dove was released and it never came back. It had found a home.

What was the raven doing all that time? The raven didn't need a tree and it didn't need to return to the ark.

SIX-FEET-DEEP THOUGHT

Dear Abby quoted someone as saying: "Never be afraid to try something new. Remember, amateurs built the ark. Professionals built the *Titanic*."

The raven could perch on the dead bodies in the water. The raven had food.

After Noah's family left the ark, God made several more promises to him:

God promised never again to interrupt the earth's seasons until the end of time (Genesis 8:21, 22). He promised never again to destroy the earth

with water (Genesis 9:11). He promised never to break those promises! And he gave us the rainbow to show us he was remembering (Genesis 9:15, 16).

It's horrible that all the people in the world were so evil they had to be destroyed. But it's comforting to know that God clearly tells us in the Bible what he expects. He doesn't just sneak up on people; he tries to save them. And it's comforting to know that God always keeps his promises.

God made many promises in the Bible. You should read them, believe them and act on them. You are alive today because, over 4,000 years ago, Noah did just that.

∽◦∾

STONE-COLD FACT

The measurements of the ark were approximately 450' long x 75' wide x 45' high. Apparently it held the record as the biggest ship ever constructed—until 1884. As for how many animals the ark could have held: it had the capacity of eight freight trains that each have 65 cars (Whitcomb and Morris, *The Genesis Flood*).

midnight tale

Once upon a midnight dreary,

While I pondered, weak and weary,

Over many a quaint and curious

Volume of forgotten lore—

While I nodded, nearly napping,

Suddenly there came a tapping,

As of some one gently rapping,

Rapping at my chamber door.

·   ·   ·   ·   ·   ·   ·   ·

Deep into that darkness peering,

Long I stood there, wondering, fearing,

Doubting, dreaming dreams no mortal

Ever dared to dream before.

·   ·   ·   ·   ·   ·   ·   ·

"Ghastly grim and ancient Raven

Wandering from the Nightly shore—

Tell me what thy lordly name is

On the Night's Plutonian shore!"

Quoth the Raven, "Nevermore."

—"The Raven" by Edgar Allen Poe, stanzas 1, 5, 8

in memory of
Noah

"Noah did everything just as God commanded him."
Genesis 6:22, NIV

The Mystery of Madam X

Here Lies
Lot's wife, the unnamed wife of Abraham's nephew

THE BODY

Tornado!

Dorothy saw it coming. She should have run straight for the cellar. But she couldn't leave Toto behind. Once she had him in tow, she searched for Auntie Em. She kept spinning around, calling out. By the time she reached the cellar, the door was already shut. Too late. So Dorothy and Toto ended up in the land of Oz—and we ended up with a great story.

It didn't work out that well for Lot's wife.

She and her family lived in Sin City—Sodom. God said he would have saved the city if there had been even ten righteous people there. But the residents of Sodom "were wicked and

cause of death
The Lord rained down fire and burning sulfur from the sky, and she became a pillar of salt (Genesis 19).

last words
No recorded words.

Ⓢ **EPITAPH** Ⓢ
Here snug in her grave my wife doth lie.
Now she's at rest, and so am I!

DEATH
SENTENCE

"I'd rather die in New York than live anywhere else."

—seen on a t-shirt

were sinning greatly" (Genesis 13:13, NIV). We know that at least part of the trouble was homosexual behavior (Genesis 19:5).

God personally sent an angel escort to get Lot and his family out.

"Hurry!" said the angel (Genesis 19:14). But Lot's son-in-law thought he was joking.

"Hurry!" said the angel to Lot (v. 15). But Lot hesitated. The angel had to take his hand!

"Don't look back," said the angel (v. 17). Then . . . all Heaven broke loose! Perhaps lightning struck a petroleum field and gases seeping up from the ground ignited into massive explosions. Perhaps there was also miraculous fire dropping from the sky . . . with a few earthquakes thrown in. Burning sulfur began to rain down. Lot's wife should have kept running. But she paused to look back.

Dorothy hesitated because of Toto and Auntie Em. They were important to her. What in Sodom was so important to Lot's wife? What was she thinking?

Well . . . maybe they had a really

SIX-FEET-DEEP THOUGHT

Lynn: *Lot's wife was really a piece of work—*
Cheryl: *—who became a piece of artwork!*

good mall. Or maybe there weren't any decent restaurants once you left the city. Their pro baseball team could've been about to win the championship—and Lot's wife just loooooooved hot dogs!

You know . . . important stuff.

The actions of Lot's wife cost her dearly. The Bible says she "became a pillar of salt" (v. 26). Archaeologists believe the location of the now-buried city is at the south end of the Dead Sea. All kinds of strange salt formations dot the area. And somewhere in all of that . . . are the remains of Lot's wife.

All because she couldn't tear herself away from a very bad place. Could anything have been *that* important? Remember, God could not even find a handful of people to save. The place was rotten. Couldn't Lot's wife see that?

Hmmm. Have you ever watched a really bad movie just to see the one or two good parts? Have you ever bought one great thing at a store that sold mostly nasty stuff?

"Well," you told yourself, "I know it's

∾∾

STONE-COLD FACT
The coat of arms of Australia features a picture of an emu, who cannot move backward because of its three-toed feet, and a kangaroo, who cannot move backward because of its long tail. Australia wants to be viewed as a forward-moving country.

kinda bad, but I really like . . . "

I'm afraid that's what Lot's wife did. To her, 95 percent bad was still OK.

But to God, it wasn't.

Think about it.

in memory of
Lot's wife

"No one who . . . looks back is fit for service in the kingdom of God."
Luke 9:62, niv

✝

SHE DIED LAUGHING

Here Lies
Sarah, wife of Abraham

THE BODY

I never cared much for Sarah. But she managed to get herself favorably written up in the books of Genesis, Isaiah, Romans, Hebrews and 1 Peter. So she must've done *something* right. Better look again.

Sarah got off to a bad start when she didn't believe God. God told Abraham he would have a son. Sarah was Abraham's wife. But since she hadn't had children so far (and she was quite old), she didn't believe she could now. She insisted Abraham sleep with her servant girl—and have a child in their household that way. Then there began a kind of rivalry between the two women, and Sarah mistreated the servant girl. I didn't like that. After all, the whole thing had been Sarah's idea in the first place.

cause of death
Unknown, at age 127 (Genesis 23:1, 2).

last words
Sarah's last recorded words were spoken long before her death. They are strong words to her husband: "Get rid of that slave woman and her son, for that slave woman's son will never share in the inheritance with my son Isaac" (Genesis 21:10, NIV).

27

Then God's spooky special messenger came (Genesis 18) to get Sarah back on track with God's plan. Sarah herself, he said, was to have the child God promised. She still didn't believe. She laughed in God's face! I didn't like that.

Sarah's baby was born. Sarah named him Isaac. And here's where we need to give Sarah another look. The name *Isaac* is from the Hebrew word for laughter. Hold that thought.

We don't read many more real details about Sarah. Isaiah calls her the mother of the Jewish people (51:2). Peter tells us she was a good wife (1 Peter 3:6).

Was her life no more than that? Seems kind of boring.

But maybe after God came through with his promise of her son, Sarah happily settled in to being a good wife and mother. As she laughed at little Isaac's childish antics, she probably recalled that she had laughed at the idea of ever having this child. Her laugh of disbelief became a laugh of pure joy. Every time she said his name she would be reminded.

life line ───∿∿∿∿∿

Several online sources tell the account of a 58-year-old woman who literally died laughing. Following a severe headache, she went into a laughing fit, which continued for two hours in spite of the doctor's efforts to stop it. Not long after, she collapsed and died.

God gives some people jobs that actually look important while they're being done. Other jobs aren't so obviously important; they may seem kind of boring. Only later is their importance seen and understood. Sarah's work was this last type. Raising one child may not seem like an exciting, important job. But God was founding a nation that began with Sarah and Abraham. So their son would be an extremely important link in the chain. I think Sarah devoted herself to raising him properly. Her efforts paid off. Isaac turned out just fine—we don't find much against him in the pages of the Bible.

SIX-FEET-DEEP THOUGHT

"The future destiny of a child is always in the hands of his mother."
—Napoleon Bonaparte

Sarah's was a calm story without a lot of drama. She was just a normal mom who lived a good life. Someday it'll be your turn to be a mom or dad. Remember Sarah. Sure, she made mistakes. But she laughed a lot and kept going. I like that.

HEART-STOPPER

"If you bungle raising your children, I don't think whatever else you do well matters very much."
—Jacqueline Kennedy Onassis

in memory of
Sarah

"God has brought me laughter."
Genesis 21:6, NIV

As Good As Dead

Here Lies
Abraham, father of a nation

THE BODY

George had a son named Alfred. Alfred married Sally. Unfortunately Alfred died, and his father George was very sad. But what happened next made him even more sad. Sally married again. And she married a very disreputable man, a scoundrel. George was enraged; this was a disgrace. Then Sally died. George was still so upset with what she had done, he refused to let her be buried in the cemetery. Today in the village of Corinth, Kentucky, there is a little cemetery with a fence around it. Outside the fence is a single grave: Sally's. I've seen it myself. George was my great-great grandfather.

cause of death

Unknown. But it must have been peaceful. He "died in a good old age, an old man, and full of years" (Genesis 25:8, KJV).

last words

His last recorded words are spoken to a servant: Do "not get a wife for my son from the daughters of the Canaanites" (Genesis 24:3, NIV).

life line ⎯⋏⋁⋀⋁⋀⋀

Abraham "was called God's friend" (James 2:23, NIV).

All parents want their sons to marry good wives. All parents want good daughters-in-law.

Abraham was no different. Abraham had a good wife in Sarah. He wanted his son Isaac to have a good wife. He knew that it is important to choose a partner wisely.

Abraham really had been too old to have a child ("as good as dead") when Isaac was born. Now he was terribly old and nearly dead. Before he died he could have asked for one more trip to Six Flags Over Ezion-geber. Or one last meal at the House of Quail. But Abraham had something much more important on his mind.

Abraham sent his servant to find a wife for Isaac. (He must have been too unwell to go himself.) He wanted a wife found from among his own people, not from among the Canaanites. The problem wasn't that the Canaanites were for-eigners. The problem was that they weren't believers in God.

Abraham wanted a daughter-in-law who followed God. Such a girl would be a good, faithful wife to Isaac. She would be an important person at the beginning of the numerous descen-

ഗ്ലാ **EPITAPH** ഗ്ലാ

Our aged father is now
   conveyed
To his long home in silence
   laid
Hast burst his cage and
   winged his way
To realms of bliss in end-
   less day.
   —in New York, died 1841

32

HEART-STOPPER

"People shop for a bathing suit with more care than they do a husband or wife."
—Erma Bombeck

dants Abraham had been promised. The servant prayed for the Lord to show him the right girl. And I imagine Abraham was praying, too, the whole time the servant was gone.

Of course, the Lord is going to help if you ask. The servant was led right to a wonderful—and beautiful—girl, Rebekah.

Abraham had spent his last energy to help his son find the right wife. Abraham became the father—and father-in-law—of a great nation.

SIX-FEET-DEEP THOUGHT

Genesis 49:29-32 tells of the burial of Abraham's daughter-in-law Rebekah. Unlike Sally in the above story, Rebekah remained in favor. She was buried near the village of Mamre— *inside* the cemetery.

midnight tale

I once received a mailing from a singles club. (I don't know why; I was married at the time!) I was to answer 38 questions that would help me find the perfect mate. Did I prefer reading or partying? What did I think about current fashion trends? Were my feelings easily hurt? There was not one word about God. I could check a little box to indicate if I was single, divorced, widowed or separated. Separated? Yeah, even people who were just thinking about divorce could go ahead and start looking for a new mate. What's wrong with this picture?

in memory of
Abraham

"And so from this one man, and he as good as dead, came descendants as numerous as the stars."

Hebrews 11:12, niv

✝ The Mummy's Return

Here Lies
Joseph, the boy slave who ruled Egypt

THE BODY

Joseph was wrapped from head to toe.

In integrity.

Integrity means having the rules of right and wrong clearly in your head—*and* living by them, no matter what. (On the vocab test, the synonym is *rectitude* and the antonym is *turpitude*.)

People without integrity try to excuse their bad behavior by saying they've had a rough life. Give me a break. Look what happened to Joseph.

When he was 17 his brothers sold him. Sold him!

He was taken to Egypt. That was a foreign country to him. Foreign language. People worshiping foreign gods. His integrity got him a position of honor in the house of the captain of Pharaoh's guard, Potiphar. His integrity made him say no when

cause of death
Unknown.

last words
His last recorded words were spoken to his brothers: "God will surely come to your aid, and then you must carry my bones up from this place" (Genesis 50:25, NIV).

Potiphar's wife came on to him.

She had him thrown in prison.

Joseph's integrity got him put in charge of the prison, second to the warden. His integrity made him help another prisoner. "Hey," Joseph told him, "when you get out, put in a good word for me to . . ."

But he forgot.

Integrity caused Joseph to help Pharaoh by interpreting his dream. And he gave God credit when he could have used his knowledge to bargain his way out of prison.

That integrity gave Joseph freedom and command of Pharaoh's palace. And it was Joseph who saved the whole land of Egypt when famine came.

Were the difficult times worth it? Absolutely.

Was Joseph's life easy? Absolutely not.

There was always a hole in Joseph's heart. He never really got over what his brothers had done. How could he? And he missed his dad. How could he not? Joseph was a normal guy.

SIX-FEET-DEEP THOUGHT

"If you have integrity, nothing else matters. If you don't have integrity, nothing else matters."

—Alan Simpson, former senator

When he finally met his brothers again, the pain came rushing back. Joseph was over 40 by that time—but he cried so loudly he could be heard all over the place.

You can read the whole story in Genesis 37, 39-50.

I think the Lord had a soft spot for Joseph. He granted Joseph's last request. Joseph wanted to go home. Oh, he knew he'd die in Egypt but he wanted to be buried at home. That's another clue about his heartache, isn't it? He had missed home all those years. But God had given Joseph a very special and exciting life. Joseph died and was embalmed Egyptian style. Then . . .

∽ **EPITAPH** ∽

Gone home.
—on the tombstones of many believers

400 years later, when all the people were led out of Egypt, headed for home, Moses "took the bones of Joseph with him" (Exodus 13:19, NIV).

Joseph's integrity is what makes him memorable. If you read his story once, you won't forget it. God didn't forget Joseph, even 400 years after he had died.

—————————————————————————————————

HEART-STOPPER
Less than 400 years ago doctors in Europe ground Egyptian mummies into powder and used it as medicine.

Gotta have the newest CD?

Gotta have the latest style sweater?

You might manage without them.

But integrity? Now there's something you've really gotta have.

 ## midnight tale

Joe's bros died a thousand deaths in the years Joseph was gone. All that time they didn't know how he ended up—or where. All that time they had guilt over what they'd done. All that time they watched their father's sadness as he missed his son. Their evil deed haunted them. Once, when something bad happened to them 20 years later, they said, "We're surely being punished for what we did to Joseph." Even after they reunited with Joseph, they were afraid he would take revenge. Poor guys. They didn't understand integrity.

in memory of
Joseph

He told his brothers, "You meant to hurt me. But God turned your evil into good . . . to save the lives of many people."
GENESIS 50:20, ICB

✝ Lost at Sea

Here Lies
Pharaoh and his army, who refused to let God's people go

THE BODY

Over the course of your life, you'll hear a number of people say, "I don't believe in God. But if I saw a miracle, I'd believe."

News flash: Don't believe *them*.

Ten different plagues (miraculous disasters) hit Egypt. (The entire account is recorded in Exodus 7–14.) Each time, Moses told Pharaoh the kind of plague that was coming. Each time, Pharaoh scoffed. Each time, the plague hit. Each time, when the plague became unbearable, Pharaoh bargained. He agreed to free Moses and his people (so the suffering would stop). Each time, the plague ended and Pharaoh broke his promise.

Don't give Pharaoh any breaks.

cause of death

While they were in the middle of the parted Red Sea, the Lord made their chariot wheels come off and threw them into confusion. Then the Red Sea waters came back into place and drowned them. (Psalm 136:15 says Pharaoh was drowned with the army.)

last words

"Let's get away from the Israelites! The LORD is fighting for them against Egypt" (Exodus 14:25, NIV).

39

He had plenty of proof about God through these miraculous disasters. And they weren't just random miracles; they were miracles with a message.

Egypt worshiped many gods. When God turned the Nile River into blood, God was overpowering Khnum the guardian of the Nile, Hopi the spirit of the Nile and Osiris whose bloodstream was the Nile.

When God sent a bazillion frogs, it was as if he were saying, "You trust in Heqt, the god of the resurrection, whose form is a frog. You think frogs can help you? Here—here are all the frogs you need."

Imhotep the god of medicine couldn't stop the plague of boils. Re (or Ra) and Horus, sun gods, could not stop the plague of darkness. And Osiris the giver of life could not stop the deaths of all the firstborn of Egypt.

With the deaths of all firstborn, Pharaoh lost his own oldest son. And he released Moses and his people. But, after the initial shock of the

EPITAPH

Here lies the body of
Jonathan Pound;
He was lost at sea and
never found.

deaths wore off, Pharaoh and his army chased them. The moment of truth was near. When Moses and the people reached the Red Sea and wondered what in the world they were going to do, the Lord sent a pillar of fire to hold Pharaoh back. Pharaoh saw it, and he saw the Red Sea part to let God's people escape. Even at the last minute he was shown two more major miracles. And still . . .

Want to see a miracle?

Look in the mirror. Look at your eye. If you visit the Grand Canyon or Niagara Falls or Mt. Rainier, you will gasp at the sight. What you are seeing with your own eye is so much more vivid than what you saw in photographs.

In thousands of years of human history no one has invented a camera that can replace your own eye. The human eye alone is enough of a miracle to prove the existence of a creative mastermind. There are many wonders all around you every day: bumblebees, Venus flytraps, Jupiter . . .

of grave concern

An odd—and sad—twist to our story: The Israelites who believed in God already, and then saw all these miracles as bonus evidence, later slipped away from following God. The Bible describes those "whose carcasses fell in the wilderness" (Hebrews 3:17, KJV). Their "bodies fell in the desert" (NIV). The Egyptians died in a sea of water, and the Israelites died in a sea of sand.

SIX-FEET-DEEP THOUGHT

Joan (to God): *OK, let's see a miracle.*

God (pointing).

Joan: *That's a tree.*

God: *Let's see YOU make one.*

—from the TV series *Joan of Arcadia*

Someday you also may see a miracle like the ones Pharaoh and his army witnessed.

In the meantime, maybe you've seen enough.

 midnight tale

Historians are not sure which pharaoh was ruling Egypt at this time. Many think it was Amenhotep II whose reign began in 1453 B.C. The epic movie *The Ten Commandments* calls the pharaoh of the exodus Rameses II (1304 B.C.). King Tut, the famous boy king whose extravagant tomb was discovered in 1922, is dated 1377 B.C.

—*Halley's Bible Handbook*

in memory of
Pharaoh and his army

"[God] sent his signs and wonders into your midst, O Egypt."
Psalm 135:9, NIV

ASHES TO ASHES

Here Lies
Nadab and Abihu, sons of the high priest Aaron

THE BODY

It was Lyle's idea.

Or maybe it was Erik's.

We'll probably never know who started it.

But one day in 1989, brothers Lyle and Erik Menendez decided the rules didn't apply to them. They murdered their parents. They are in prison for life.

It was Nadab's idea.

Or maybe it was Abihu's.

We'll probably never know who started it. But one day around 1300 B.C., brothers Nadab and Abihu decided the rules didn't apply to them. They didn't light the fire of God's altar in the way he'd instructed. They got fire, all right. They were cremated on the spot.

cause of death
"Fire came out from the presence of the LORD and consumed them"
(Leviticus 10:2, NIV).

last words
No recorded words.

What Nadab and Abihu did doesn't seem to be a very big deal. So what if they got fire from a different place? Maybe they even peeked into the forbidden holy of holies. So what? That's exactly the point. *They* were deciding which of God's rules were a big deal and which weren't.

I guess that's what Lyle and Erik did too.

But you can't do that. God's rules are God's rules. We don't have the option of listing them in our order of importance, obeying the top four and tossing the rest.

God hit hard in some of the Old Testament stories—partly to show us that he means business. With Nadab and Abihu . . . well, everything about the Old Testament worship system was a symbol of what Jesus would later do for us. It was serious. It was sacred. The altar for offering lamb sacrifices represented the cross on which Jesus, the Lamb of God, would be sacrificed—much later—for all sins.

"But," you say, "Nadab and Abihu couldn't have known that." That's right, they didn't.

All they needed to know was what they *did* know: they knew that God is in charge of the world. And they knew his commands about the altar.

SIX-FEET-DEEP THOUGHT

"God will never reveal more truth about himself till you obey what you know already."

—Oswald Chambers

All Lyle and Erik needed to know was what they *did* know: they knew that God is in charge of the world. And they knew his commands about murder.

Lyle and Erik and Nadab and Abihu messed with God. You can't do that. It's not fun and it doesn't pay.

All you need to know is what you already know: God is in charge of the world. And you have all his commands in the Bible.

Tell your brothers and sisters.

And . . . step away from the fire.

EPITAPH

Here lies what's left
of Leslie Moore.
No Les.
No More.

—unknown

HEART-STOPPER

Around 620 B.C., a lawmaker named Draco wrote *Laws on Murder*. He ordered execution for all crimes . . . even laziness.

midnight tale

"Diamonds are forever. And now you can be too," reported *Reader's Digest* (July 2003). A new company can pull out carbon from cremated remains. The application of heat and pressure (and your payment of a few thousand bucks) turns those remains into diamonds. The company vice president said, "It isn't in memory of a loved one, it *is* the loved one."

in memory of
Nadab and Abihu

"There is a path before each person that seems right,
but it ends in death."

Proverbs 14:12, NLT

Abra Cadaver

Here Lies
Moses, the deliverer

THE BODY

"Abracadabra."

"Hocus-pocus."

"One-two-three and . . . *poof!*"

"I'll tap three times with my magic wand."

Magic words. Magic shows. We love it all: the card tricks, the beautiful girl being sawed in two, the dove emerging from the handkerchief . . . why, David Copperfield even made the Statue of Liberty disappear.

The life of Moses was one long magic show.

The first trick occurred when Moses was an infant. He was one of thousands

cause of death

Unknown. He died alone on Mt. Nebo, and God secretly buried his body somewhere else (Deuteronomy 34:1, 5, 6).

last words

The last recorded words were spoken *to*, not *by*, Moses. The Lord showed him the promised land and said, "I have let you see it with your eyes, but you will not cross over into it" (Deuteronomy 34:4, NIV). Perhaps Moses responded, "Missed it by *that* much."

47

WORDS TO LIVE BY

"[God] performs wonders that cannot be fathomed, miracles that cannot be counted."

Job 5:9, NIV

~ **EPITAPH** ~

Lives of great men all remind us
We can make our lives sublime,
And, departing, leave behind us
Footprints on the sands of time.

—Henry Wadsworth Longfellow

of Israelites living in slavery in Egypt. When Egyptian rulers felt the Israelites were becoming too numerous, the boy babies of Israel were ordered killed. Moses' mother hid baby Moses in a basket floating in the river and . . . *poof!* The next thing we know, an Egyptian princess rescued him and raised him in the palace! Moses was the one to whom God spoke from a burning bush. He called down the ten plagues on Egypt. He raised his staff— and the Red Sea parted.

But Moses didn't strut on the stage of his life with a black cape and a confident smile for the crowd. In fact, he tried to get out of the whole performance.

When God first asked Moses to be his rep—to go to Egypt and stand up to Pharaoh—Moses hid his face. He didn't even want to discuss it. He had quite an argument with God in Exodus 3, 4. Here's Moses' side of it:

"I'm not able to do that."

"I don't have any real authority."

DEATH SENTENCE

"You shall not misuse the name of the LORD your God."

Exodus 20:7, NIV

"What if they don't listen?"

"I'm not a very good speaker."

"Oh, God, could you just send someone else?"

Finally, he followed God. And while he was following God, he leaned *on* God. One day, though, he got a little full of himself. In Numbers 20 God told him to speak to a rock and water would come out for the people to drink. But Moses didn't do exactly what God said. He spoke to the *people:* "Must we bring you water out of this rock?" (We?) Then he raised his "magic wand" and hit the rock twice. You can almost see him flinging his black cape. The Amazing Moses. He temporarily forgot that God was the real magician and he was only the lovely assistant.

We need to remember that ourselves. Any "magic" in our lives is the result of God's working his marvels through the gifts he has given to us.

life line

"I don't know if God wept at Moses' funeral. . . . I don't know who will bury me. . . . But I look back over the moments of my life and see the hands that carried Moses to his grave lifting me out of mine."

—Rich Mullins (died 1997)

STONE-COLD FACT
Moses' greatest fear—speaking in public—is shared by a large percentage of the population. There is even a book out entitled *I'd Rather Die Than Give a Speech*.

HEART-STOPPER

Meredith's Book of Lists names 38 miracles associated with the life of Moses.

Overall, Moses was a humble servant of God. Jesus often referred favorably to Moses. At the time of Jesus' transfiguration (Luke 9), Jesus' appearance became bright. Moses and Elijah, long dead, appeared with him and talked with him.

Moses' life with the Lord was . . . well, magic.

 ## midnight tale

Many religions, as well as occult rituals, use "magic words." I'm not going to write any of them here. They're fake. The Lord doesn't like our using them. If there is a real magic word in the Bible it's: I AM. When Moses wondered what authority he had to make Egypt listen, God told him to say that he was sent by I AM (Exodus 3:13, 14). The Hebrew word for that may be the same root for the word *Lord, Jehovah.* God's name. I AM. No one caused God to exist. He just is. He is who he is. He is because he is.

More than 1,000 years after Moses, soldiers were looking for Jesus in order to arrest him. When Jesus said, "I AM he," they fell over backwards (John 18:4-6).

If you belong to the Lord you have the power that comes with wearing his name. There will come a day when everyone will bow before "the name that is above every name" (Philippians 2:9, 10, NIV).

in memory of
Moses

"Our help is in the name of the LORD."
Psalm 124:8, NIV

PURPLE HEART

Here Lies
Joshua, victorious commander of Israel

THE BODY

Bushido. The way of the warrior.

Bushido was the code of conduct followed by the samurai of old Japan. Samurai were to have courage, truth, honor, loyalty.

When the Lord commissioned Joshua to take over for Moses, he gave Joshua a code to live by. It makes me think of bushido:

"Be strong and very courageous. . . . Meditate on [my law] day and night, so that you may be careful to do everything written in it. Then you will be prosperous and successful. . . . Do not be terrified; do not be discouraged, for the LORD your God will be with you" (Joshua 1:7-9, NIV).

It's all there: courage, truth, honor, loyalty.

cause of death

Unknown. He gave a final speech urging the people to remain true to God, and he died at age 110 (Joshua 24:29).

last words

His very last words are not known. But his most famous words are from his final recorded speech: "Choose for yourselves this day whom you will serve. . . . As for me and my household, we will serve the LORD" (Joshua 24:15, NIV).

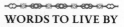

life line

"When placed in command—take charge."

—General Norman Schwarzkopf

Samurai were under their *daimyo,* or feudal lords. The outstanding daimyo became *shogun,* the leader of Japan's military. The spiritual head of the shogun was the emperor himself, called the heavenly ruler, descendant of the sun goddess Amaterasu.

Joshua was under . . .

Joshua was leading his troops to capture Jericho (in the famous event that brought the city walls down in Joshua 6). Near Jericho he had a briefing with his commander. What's strange is that Joshua didn't *have* a commander!

Nevertheless, a "man" with a drawn sword appeared. Some biblical scholars think it may have been Michael the archangel. Others think it was an appearance of Jesus himself—long before he came to Earth as a baby. The commander told Joshua that he was on holy ground (Joshua 5:13-15). I think he was reminding Joshua that it was God's battle, that God was present, that Joshua

STONE-COLD FACT

The Purple Heart is awarded today only to those who are wounded or killed in action. But the Military Order of the Purple Heart began in order to honor any outstanding performance in the line of duty. Joshua's role as an outstanding commander certainly qualified him as a Purple Heart. He also had a heart of gold!

was merely God's agent.

Joshua got it.

Joshua, human commander of the Lord's army, had many victories. They're recorded in the book of Joshua. Joshua was victorious because he followed the code God gave him. Joshua was shogun.

The Japanese samurai warriors with their bushido make a fascinating study. But at the top of the ranks of samurai, daimyo and shogun is only the mythical sun goddess. *Joshua-do,* the way of Joshua, is superior:

Living with courage in the Lord's presence.

Following the way of God's law.

Honor, pride, purpose.

And loyalty to the true ruler of Heaven, the Lord Almighty.

HEART-STOPPER

"Without an acknowledgement of God, I cannot do my duty."

—Alabama Judge Roy Moore, who installed a 5,000-pound granite monument of the Ten Commandments in the state judiciary building, then was arrested for refusing to remove it.

midnight tale

The first sword in the Bible appears in Genesis 3:24. After Adam and Eve were expelled from the Garden of Eden, the Lord placed angels with flaming swords as guards so they couldn't get back in.

in memory of
Joshua

*"It is not by sword or spear that the L*ORD *saves;*
*for the battle is the L*ORD*'s."*
1 Samuel 17:47, NIV

✠ Midnight Warrior

Here Lies

Gideon, the judge-warrior who defeated the Midianites

THE BODY

One type of suicide mission involves people deliberately blowing themselves up in order to also take out the enemy.

Another type is really a joking use of the term—when someone tries a stunt so outlandish there's not much chance of survival. You know, people who want to go over Niagara Falls in a barrel or want to catapult across the Grand Canyon. Or like the time you and your friends thought you could jump off your roof, onto the trampoline, over the fence and into the Watsons' swimming pool. Suicide mission.

Then there's the kind of suicide mission Gideon was on.

cause of death
Unknown. Gideon "died at a good old age" (Judges 8:32, NIV).

last words
His last recorded words were spoken after he was victorious over the Midianites. He refused to govern the Israelites, saying, "The LORD will rule over you" (Judges 8:23, NIV).

The Midianites oppressed the Israelites. They invaded the land. They took or destroyed everything. The Bible says they were like a swarm of locusts—you couldn't count them (Judges 6:5).

Then God chose Gideon as the Israelite warrior to lead the uprising against the Midianites. But Gideon's clan was the least powerful of his tribe. And he was an unimportant person in that clan. Gideon smelled disaster. (Perhaps he recalled his childhood when he missed the Watsons' swimming pool by a mile and landed in their award-winning rose bushes. Suicide mission.)

The Midianite army and their allies numbered about 15,000 at this point, after God's army had wiped out 120,000 of them (Judges 8:10). Originally Gideon had managed to gather 32,000 men (Judges 7). Then God said that was too many soldiers. Too many?! All who were afraid were excused. Exit 22,000. Gideon must have been shaking, but God said there were still too many. They were given a little test which reduced the ranks to a mere 300 men. *Gulp.* Kind of like the battle for Helm's Deep in *The Lord of the Rings: The Two*

Towers. But God really likes odds like that.

Gideon's army won. With trumpets, jars and torches.

Gideon and his men sneaked close to the enemy in the middle of the night with the jars covering their torches. At the signal they blasted their trumpets and broke their jars. If you've ever been jolted awake by a horrific sound, you can imagine: the trumpets must have shattered every nerve. The sounds of all those jars breaking magnified the effect. Then . . . flashing lights everywhere!

The poor Midianites started attacking each other and running away.

Sometimes God asks us to do the impossible. But really he's asking us to let him do his thing through us. God doesn't need any weapons and he doesn't need large numbers of people. He doesn't need our help.

Remember Gideon—

Frightened midnight warrior.

Warrior in service to the Most High.

midnight tale

God told Gideon to tear down the altar to the false gods and rebuild his, God's, altar. Gideon obeyed. But because he was afraid of all the people, he did it at night (Judges 6:25-32).

in memory of
Gideon

"[the Lord's] power is made perfect in weakness. . . .
When I am weak, then I am strong."
2 Corinthians 12:9, 10, niv

Let's Roll!

Here Lies
Samson, judge of Israel

THE BODY

Her husband was a congressman for the North. He didn't know his wife, Eugenia, was a spy for the South. She had even joined Rose Greenhow's Civil War spy ring. The ladies got information; they hid things under their big hoop skirts. At one point Rose was imprisoned but continued her work from there.

Yes, there were lady spies in the Civil War days. There have always been lady spies. All lady spies have spunk. But there's something else they have in common: charm. They'd have to have charm. That's how they manage to learn secrets from men. (Pay attention, guys!)

Eugenia and Rose were charming; you can count on it. Sidney Bristow, the fictional agent on TV's *Alias,* has charm. And long ago, the very real Delilah had it.

cause of death
He shifted the two central pillars of the temple of the false god Dagon and caused the temple to collapse, killing himself and 3,000 Philistines (Judges 16:27, 29, 30).

last words
"Let me die with the Philistines!" (Judges 16:30, NIV).

Delilah, on behalf of the Philistines, used her charms against Samson.

Samson's account is recorded in Judges 13-16.

He had been set apart before birth as the person who would begin to deliver Israel from the Philistines. As an outward sign of his special relationship with God, he was to avoid drinking alcohol and he was never to cut his hair.

Samson definitely had a wild side. He tore a lion apart with his bare hands; using a jawbone as a weapon, he attacked a group of men; and then there were the flaming foxes . . .

Even so, the strong man with long hair is listed in the Hebrews 11 faith chapter. So we have to assume that his basic character was good.

But Samson's weakness involved "ladies with charm."

He had been married before—to a charming lady. Samson had made a little bet with some friends. The friends plotted with Samson's wife to get her to find out the secret. She used a line that we still hear today, "If you really loved me, you'd tell me!" He finally did. It's not a happy story.

⟨⟨⟨ EPITAPH ⟩⟩⟩

My friend judge me not,
Thou seest I judge not
    thee;
Betwixt the stirrup and the
    ground,
Mercy I ask'd, mercy I
    found.

Then we find Samson again in the same situation. Delilah was a charming lady spying for the Philistines. They played a little teasing game as she tried to learn the secret of his strength. He should have known better. But finally he told Delilah the secret was his long hair. Not only did the Philistines rush in and cut his hair, they gouged out his eyes and gave him an embarrassing job (Judges 16:21)—in public where everyone could laugh at him. (Pay attention, guys!)

But Samson was obviously sorry. And he was willing to die to make things right again. We must try to avoid doing stupid things. But when we fail, God is always waiting to take us back and make things right.

of grave concern

The Nazis exterminated thousands of people in the gas chambers of the Auschwitz concentration camp in Poland. Other prisoners were required to shave the hair of the dead. The hair was packed up and shipped to Germany where it was to be woven into nice clothes for upper-class citizens.

—information from a tour guide

life line —⋀⋀⋀⋀⋀

Did you know that you can sell your long hair to be made into wigs for people who have lost their hair due to cancer treatments?

∽∾∽

STONE-COLD FACT

Samson's strength was not actually in Samson's hair itself. His strength was in his relationship with God. The long hair symbolized that relationship. When he put himself in a position where the enemy could cut his hair, it showed that he was not being careful about his relationship with God.

Take a look at *your* weaknesses. If you turn them over to God, you can be sure that he will empower you with his strength.

 ## midnight tale

The worst mass murder in U.S. history, according to *The Guinness Book of World Records*, occurred in 1990. It was an act of revenge. A man had been thrown out of a club for his bad behavior. To get even, the man set fire to the place and 87 people died.

in memory of
Samson

His "weakness was turned to strength."

Hebrews 11:34, NIV

✝ Terror at Shiloh Gate

Here Lies
Eli, high priest and judge of Israel

The Body

Eli was a gentle soul.

It was he who raised the boy Samuel. Samuel's mother dedicated him to God and placed him in the care of the priest Eli. Under Eli's care, Samuel grew to become the last and greatest judge of Israel.

Eli may have been too gentle. His own two sons were very wicked and disobedient. They needed a firm hand. But Eli (according to 1 Samuel 2) settled for mild rebukes, along the lines of: "Now, now, boys, I'm hearing naughty things about you."

The day Eli died, he was waiting at the city gate. Waiting for news about the battle between his people the Israelites and the Philistines.

cause of death
At age 98, upon being told that the ark of the covenant had been captured, he fell backward off his chair and broke his neck (1 Samuel 4:15-18).

last words
"What happened?" (1 Samuel 4:16, NLT).

63

He received two dreaded messages: 1) His sons had been killed. 2) The ark of the covenant had been taken.

Nothing is said about Eli's reaction to the news of his sons' deaths. What terrified him was the news about the ark. So we need to understand the significance of the ark.

The ark of the covenant (which looked just like the one in the movie *Raiders of the Lost Ark*) represented the presence of God. Today, if you are a member of God's family, God lives in your heart. In Jesus' day, there was a great temple in Jerusalem. Going to the temple to worship put the worshipers formally in God's presence. But in Eli's day, things were different. The "temple" was a portable tent-like structure called a tabernacle. As the Israelites moved around, they could easily dismantle it and set it up again. There were various elements to the tabernacle. But the most important one was the ark of the covenant. There were specific rules about the ark: how to carry it, who could approach it. Wherever the ark went, God went. God with us.

The ark was carried when Joshua and his troops conquered Jericho. Israel's enemies wanted the ark. (Of course, the enemies were mistaken about the ark. They thought it had power within itself. They didn't understand that you actually had to be on God's side for the power of the ark to work.)

The ark of the covenant meant everything to Eli, because being in the Lord's presence meant everything to Eli. After all, he had been the Lord's priest for many years.

And so, that fateful day, he sat at Shiloh Gate, waiting for news from the battle. It was bad news. The ark of the covenant was gone. God's presence had left Israel. The news killed Eli.

What was true for Eli is true for us today: God's presence in our lives is the very thing that gives meaning to all of life. God with us.

of grave concern

The account of Eli says he was quite heavy when he died. The fascinating death of another overweight man is recorded in Judges 3:17, 21, 22. King Eglon of Moab was "a very fat man." An assassin named Ehud approached the king, pretending to be on a peaceful mission. But Ehud plunged his sword into the king's fat belly. "Even the handle sank in after the blade" (NIV).

ᏆᎯᏆ EPITAPH ᏆᎯᏆ

Now I lay me down to
    sleep,
I pray the Lord my soul to
    keep;
And if I die before I wake,
I pray the Lord my soul to
    take.

— the famous children's
    prayer, first known to
    be in print in 1737

midnight tale

If you recall, Indiana Jones was very careful how he carried the ark of the covenant. That caution was right out of the Bible. The ark was to be carried with long poles that fit through rings on the ark. It wasn't to be touched. On one occasion (2 Samuel 6:1-8), the Israelites didn't do that—they just placed the ark on a cart. First mistake. Then the oxen pulling the cart stumbled. A man named Uzzah reached out (Oh, no! Don't touch it!) and touched the ark to steady it. Second mistake. He died on the spot. I guess he hadn't seen the movie.

in memory of
Eli

"Uphold me and set me in your presence forever.
Praise be to the LORD."
Psalm 41:12, 13, NIV

The Bigger They Are, the Harder They Fall

Here Lies
Goliath, champion Philistine warrior

THE BODY

"We'll have to get Sam," the tired farmer said.

The cows were running wild. Several attempts to get them into the barn had failed. You wouldn't think it likely that Sam could help. He was what some people might call the village idiot. But he had one very useful talent—though it wasn't needed often. Sam could buzz like a warble fly.

Sam arrived in the cow pasture. And, with a couple of very believable *MmmmBbbbzzzzzz*es, the alarmed cows headed straight for the shelter of the barn. (Told in *All Creatures Great and Small* by James Herriot.)

I picture Goliath as a Sam-type. I can imagine him as a child—

cause of death

He was hit in the forehead with one stone from David's slingshot and, apparently, was finished off with his own sword.

last words

His last recorded words were spoken to David. "Come here," he said, "and I'll give your flesh to the birds of the air and the beasts of the field!" (1 Samuel 17:44, NIV).

DEATH
SENTENCE

*If the stone only stunned the
giant, maybe he managed to
say one more thing as he
toppled over. Maybe
Goliath's real last words
were: "Uh . . . don't forget to
feed the cat."*

—Arian Armstrong

shouting "Boo!" at babies, tying cats' tails together, skipping school to break windows in Old Man Kelsey's greenhouse. Then, whenever the other kids needed to have someone whacked, they called Goliath. I think whacking may have been Goliath's only talent. You can almost hear the other mothers whispering, "The poor boy—it's about the only thing he's good at."

If you have only one talent, that's OK. But you have to use it properly. You have to use it for God. When you're on God's team, God does something amazing: he multiplies what you do. And he gives you other talents to use.

If Goliath had used his size and strength for God, God would have blessed him. Goliath could have become the favorite worker in the babies' class, 'cause his big arms could have rocked six babies to sleep at once. His pedigreed cats could have taken the blue ribbons at the International Feline Fest. He could have delivered heavy boxes of plants for Old Man Kelsey and earned money for college.

EPITAPH

Here lays Butch
We planted him raw
He was quick on the
   trigger
But slow on the draw.

—on a tombstone from
the old West

68

But Goliath didn't do that. He took his one talent and signed up for the wrong team—the team that was fighting God.

It wasn't actually a stone or a sword that killed Goliath. David used those, but he wasn't counting on them—and he certainly wasn't the force behind them. Goliath had all the visible weapons: his coat of armor alone weighed about 125 pounds and the point of his spear, about 15 pounds (1 Samuel 17:4-7). But as David went out, he said to Goliath, "You come to me with sword, spear, and javelin, but I come to you in the name of the LORD Almighty" (1 Samuel 17:45, NLT). The Lord brought Goliath down.

Goliath counted on his own power and his own weapons—and they were awesome. But Goliath was doomed. He was playing on the wrong side. Poor boy.

∽∾

STONE-COLD FACT

First Samuel 17:4 says Goliath was over 9' tall. *Unger's Bible Dictionary* says skeletons that tall have been found. A man over 7 1/2' tall is mentioned in 1 Chronicles 11:23. We don't know the height of the pagan King Og (who ruled 60 cities), but his bed was more than 13' long (Deuteronomy 3:11).

in memory of
Goliath

"Pride goes before destruction, a haughty spirit before a fall."
Proverbs 16:18, NIV

DEATH WISH

Here Lies
Saul, Israel's first king

THE BODY

If we'd all been at a birthday party for King Saul, and it came time for him to make a wish and blow out the candles . . . we'd still be sitting there.

Saul was a man who didn't know what he wanted. He was unfocused. His whole life was kind of a jumble. (Read his story in 1 Samuel 9–31.)

He was an impressive, tall-dark-and-handsome type. People liked him. *So far, so good.* But on the day Saul was to be introduced as king, he couldn't be found. His whereabouts were revealed in 1 Samuel 10:22: "He has hidden himself among the baggage" (NIV). *A coward?* But then he bravely marshaled the troops and won a battle. He even gave God credit for

cause of death

After he was critically wounded in battle, he begged his armor bearer to kill him. When the armor bearer refused, Saul fell on his own sword. He did not want to be left alive for the enemy. The armor bearer then killed himself (1 Samuel 31:3-6).

last words

To his armor bearer: "Take your sword and kill me before these pagan Philistines run me through and humiliate me" (1 Samuel 31:4, NLT).

The Lord said, "I know all the things you do, that you are neither hot nor cold. I wish you were one or the other! But since you are like lukewarm water, I will spit you out of my mouth!"

Revelation 3:15, 16, NLT

STONE-COLD FACT
"I don't know the key to success, but the key to failure is trying to please everybody."

—Bill Cosby

the victory. *OK, we're good now.* Wait. He violated God's laws about the sacrifices. Then he made a stupid rule that put his soldiers in danger—and threatened to kill his own son who didn't keep the rule. (King Saul's own men rescued the son.) *We're going downhill fast here.*

The Lord told King Saul to destroy everybody and everything in a battle against the Amalekites. But he kept some things. He had the nerve to say that he *had* carried out God's orders— that his soldiers only kept a few things to sacrifice to God. *Oh, brother.* Finally, though, he admitted he had sinned. *Good move.*

King Saul liked David who had come to work for him. Then the king became jealous after David's victory over Goliath . . . and tried to kill him. *Slipping again.*

But King Saul could tell God was with David, and he was afraid of the young man. *Thinking clearly now.* He promised one of his daughters in

life line
"Do or do not. There is no try."
—Yoda, *Star Wars*

marriage to David if David fought well (actually hoping he'd be killed in battle). *Oops.*

He made several attempts on David's life.

"Everybody's against me," he pouted. "Even the priests. Kill them! Kill them all!" *Really losing it now.* But his own people knew better than to do that.

After David had a chance at revenge and didn't take it, King Saul cried and apologized to David. *Well, now, maybe he's finally getting it together.*

King Saul sought the Lord's advice. *Yeah!* But he also consulted a medium (1 Samuel 28:7). *Aaarrrggghhh!*

Do you see what I mean about King Saul? I don't think he knew who he was or where he was going. He wasn't focused. His behavior was all over the place. Even Saul's death was a jumble. Was it a murder or a suicide?

I hope you'll read his story in the Bible—even though it'll give you a headache. You'll see that Saul's life would have gone so much better if he'd stayed focused on God. Is your

DEATH SENTENCE

"It's not that I'm afraid to die. I just don't want to be there when it happens."
—Woody Allen

SIX-FEET-DEEP THOUGHT

"Heartthrobs are a dime a dozen."
—heartthrob Brad Pitt

life a jumble or are you focused on God? Close your eyes for a second and think about your own life. Now, make a wish . . . and blow out the candles.

 ## midnight tale

"Japanese Family: Murder-Suicide," announced the newspaper in a small Ohio town. Police had found the parents and two small children dead in their home, with the car running in the garage. It wasn't an accident. The Japanese community was enraged at the newspaper's use of the English word *murder*. The Japanese wording would be different. When two lovers kill themselves together, it's *shinjyuu*, a double suicide. In the case of this family, the words would be *muri shinjyuu*, a forced double (or multiple) suicide. Not murder. No crime committed. It's all in how you look at things. The American Christian culture affects the English language. The Japanese non-Christian culture affects the Japanese language.

in memory of
Saul

"You acted foolishly. . . . [The LORD] would have established your kingdom over Israel for all time. But now your kingdom will not endure"
1 Samuel 13:13, 14, NIV

A Matter of Life and Death

Here Lies
Abigail and Nabal, a most unlikely couple

THE BODY

His eyes were intensely blue. Fascinating. She heard him pray with a group of students, and she liked what she heard. He prayed sincerely, confidently, but with no hint of a holier-than-thou attitude. The more she saw, the more she realized this was a man who knew God well. Later he invited her to a concert. That night, kneeling in her room, she prayed: "God, if you let me serve you with that man, I'd consider it the greatest privilege in my life." God let her do just that. In 1943 Ruth married Billy Graham. (Information from *Christian Reader*, Mar/Apr '98.)

In contrast, there's the story of Abigail and Nabal.

cause of death

Abigail—Unknown. Nabal—When Abigail told him how she'd smoothed over his bad behavior toward David, "his heart failed him . . . About ten days later, the LORD struck Nabal and he died" (1 Samuel 25:36-38, NIV).

last words

Abigail— "I'm ready to wash the feet of my master's servants" (1 Samuel 25:41, ICB). Nabal— "I have meat that I killed for my servants. . . . But I won't give it to men I don't know" (1 Samuel 25:11, ICB).

life line ⎯⋀⋀⋀⋀⋀
Outwit.
Outplay.
Outlast.

—motto of the TV
series *Survivor*

Abigail may have skipped the part about kneeling in prayer regarding her future mate. She married Nabal. And, while the Bible tells only this one story about the couple, I get the feeling that Abigail had nothing but trouble with Nabal. When you read 1 Samuel 25, you see how quickly and wisely Abigail acted in the crisis Nabal created. Probably she'd had plenty of practice cleaning up after Nabal's behavior on other occasions.

David was not yet king, though he had been appointed next in line. He and his soldiers worked for King Saul. They had protected the area from invaders; the area included Nabal's property.

On this particular day, David and his men were near Nabal's home. David sent soldiers ahead to ask Nabal if he'd extend hospitality to them and feed them. But Nabal's answer was hostile: "David? I don't know any David. Why should I share with people from who-knows-where?"

As David's servants returned to report this refusal to him, one of Nabal's servants ran and snitched to Abigail.

SIX-FEET-DEEP THOUGHT

An old superstition says it's bad luck if a bride and groom meet a funeral procession.

76

"Abigail lost no time," the Bible says. She quickly packed up a giant picnic and headed for David's camp. It was a good thing too, because David, upon hearing Nabal's message, was furious and prepared to attack him.

David and Abigail met. Abigail got off her donkey and bowed before David. She apologized, even though she herself hadn't done anything wrong. She begged David to overlook Nabal's stupidity. She even advised him to avoid any needless bloodshed, so that he would have a clear conscience when he ascended the throne.

David thanked her, accepted her gifts—and took her advice! He sent her home in peace. The next day she told Nabal what had happened. He died soon after.

Not only did Abigail save untold numbers of people, David sent for her to become his wife. And she did.

The moral of the story is this: You can't control the behavior of others. But when your companion does something foolish, run to your king. Run to King Jesus.

There's Abigail. And there's Nabal. Know the difference. It's a matter of life and death.

EPITAPH

She always did her best.
He never did.

—on an actual tombstone of a modern-day couple

in memory of
Abigail and Nabal

Those "who have already died will live again. Some of them will wake up to have life forever. But some will wake up to find shame and disgrace forever."

Daniel 12:2, ICB

HAIR TODAY—
GONE TOMORROW

Here Lies
Absalom, third son of King David

THE BODY

He had it all. He was rich, handsome and popular. And then . . . he overdosed on drugs. Or he was caught shoplifting. Or he murdered his girlfriend.

We hear Hollywood headlines like that all the time. We shake our heads, thinking, *If I had everything he had, I'd be happy. I'd never do anything like that.*

If you had lived during Old Testament times, you probably would have felt the same way about Absalom. He could have been voted *People* magazine's "Sexiest Man of the Year." He could have won the Oscar for Best Actor. Absalom had everything—but it wasn't enough. It never is.

cause of death

While riding a mule, Absalom's hair got caught in a tree branch. He hung there as the mule ran on. General Joab thrust three javelins into his heart, then ten armor bearers finished the job (2 Samuel 18:8-15).

last words

Absalom was getting advice from two sources on how to overthrow his father. His last known words were, "The advice of Hushai . . . is better than that of Ahithophel" (2 Samuel 17:14, NIV).

STONE-COLD FACT
The three leading causes of teen deaths are accidents, murders and suicides.

His is a complicated story. The part leading up to his death is told in 2 Samuel 15-18 and goes like this:

Absalom wanted to be king. But there already was a king—his father David. Never mind that. Absalom had ways. He was extremely good-looking and flashy. He cruised around town in a 1000 B.C. convertible chariot with 50 cool drivers alongside. When people came to talk with him, he kissed their hands. He attracted a lot of attention and a lot of fans.

Absalom spread criticism about King David—and broke his father's heart.

He asked Hushai and Ahithophel for advice on how to best overthrow the

DEATH
SENTENCE

Some people keep a lock of hair from a loved one who has died, especially in the case of a child's death. The hair may be pressed in a card, tied with a ribbon or put in a tiny locket. Absalom was known for his thick, heavy hair. His cut hair weighed between three and six pounds (depending on which commentary you check). See 2 Samuel 14:25, 26.

king. I guess if you're going to over-throw the king, it's a good thing to get advice. But Hushai and Ahithophel were supposed to be *King David's* loyal advisers, not Absalom's. Apparently Hushai and Ahithophel were not totally satisfied in service to King David. Perhaps they thought they could do better by latching on to the young prince. *("This guy is going places!")*

And King David, dreading a possible confrontation with his own son, left town.

Ahithophel's advice was for Absalom to sleep with David's servant girls and then gather some men to go after the king. I'm not sure how that was supposed to help. But Absalom liked the idea and *did* sleep with the servant girls—right on the rooftop in front of everybody. But he didn't take Ahithophel's advice about the revolt.

of grave concern

The handsome 1950s teen idol James Dean said he wanted to "live fast, die young, and leave a good-looking corpse." He died in a car accident at age 24.

⟨⟨⟨⟩⟩ EPITAPH ⟨⟨⟨⟩⟩

Hanged by mistake.

—found on a tombstone
from the era when
hanging was a form of
capital punishment

SIX-FEET-DEEP THOUGHT

"Think like me, and every-thing will be fine."

—Madonna

HEART-STOPPER

"The eye that mocks a father . . . will be pecked out by the ravens of the valley."
Proverbs 30:17, NIV

Hushai advised the prince to wait until all of Israel was behind Absalom and then strike. So Absalom's supporters went through some sort of ceremony to install him as king and gather a big following. Then they were off to track down and eliminate King David. The sad king-father knew this would happen, and he had been preparing for the inevitable. There was a battle. Absalom's side was defeated, and Absalom rode away to escape . . . ducking under a low-hanging tree branch in the road. And then he was gone.

"My son, my son Absalom!" King David cried. "If only I had died instead of you" (2 Samuel 18:33, NIV).

Absalom broke his father's heart.

Absalom broke his heavenly Father's heart too.

 ## midnight tale

In 1908 Crown Prince Luis Filipe was named King Dom Luis III of Portugal and reigned for . . . about 20 minutes. Assassins fatally wounded him and his father at the same time.

in memory of
Absalom

"My child, respect the Lord and the king. Don't join those people who refuse to obey them. The Lord and the king will quickly destroy such people. Those two can cause great trouble!"
Proverbs 24:21, 22, ICB

✝ SHADOW OF DEATH

Here Lies
David, Israel's most loved king

THE BODY

David started making a difference at a very young age. As a shepherd boy, he passed the quiet times in the fields by writing songs. Little did he know those songs would soon be sung by thousands of believers—and would continue to be sung for thousands of years. (But out in the fields the occasional shadow of a wild animal appeared, endangering his flocks, and David had to do battle.)

Then David became King Saul's personal musician to soothe the king during his times of depression. (But the shadow of Goliath the Philistine giant endangered the peace of the nation, and he had to do battle.)

cause of death

Unknown. When he knew he was about to die, David gave Prince Solomon some final instructions. "Then David died and was buried with his ancestors in Jerusalem. He had ruled over Israel 40 years" (1 Kings 2:10, ICB).

last words

Second Samuel 23:1-7 says "these are the last words of David." The best part is, "The person who rules righteously, who rules in the fear of God, he is like the light of the morning" (vv. 3, 4, NLT).

David was a powerful and loyal soldier for King Saul. (But the shadow of King Saul's jealousy followed him and threatened his life. David had to do battle with Satan to keep himself in line. Otherwise he would have attacked the king in retaliation.)

Eventually, David became Israel's king, the most loved of all. He followed God and ruled well. (But the shadow of temptation got too close, and David made the biggest mistake of his life. He didn't do battle with that temptation. David took another man's wife and arranged for her husband to be killed. Then David had to battle with his own guilt and shame.)

Something or someone was always lurking in the shadows to bring David down.

Dark shadows. But behind every shadow is a light. Behind all the shadows in David's life there was light—with a capital *L*. The Lord God. The light of the universe. God was the light of David's life. He wants to be that for you as well.

David's most famous Psalm 23 tells us all the secrets of life. Read it.

David was a shepherd who saw the Lord as his shepherd. Do you need someone to guide you through the rough terrain of life?

David saw the Lord as his protection from evil. Anything you need protection from?

David saw the Lord as the one who would restore him. Is there some area of life in which you need restoration?

David saw himself in eternity with the Lord. How about you?

David saw the light. So can you!

of grave concern

"Death is a shadow that always follows the body."

—old English proverb

life line —/\/\/\/\/\—

Sunlight takes 8.3 minutes to reach Earth. Son-light travels faster.

SIX-FEET-DEEP THOUGHT

"It is impossible to rightly govern our country or the world without God and the Bible."

—President George Washington on the day of his inauguration

HEART-STOPPER

"The center of God's will is not a safe place but the most dangerous place in the world. God fears nothing and no one. . . . To live outside God's will puts us in danger, but to live in His will makes us dangerous."

—Erwin McManus

midnight tale

Silly kid. He was only 12—and he thought he could make a difference in the government? But he did. In 1959 a 12-year-old boy suggested to Ohio lawmakers that they should adopt his idea for a state motto. They accepted the idea, and today you can see Matthew 19:26 set in the sidewalk leading to the steps at the statehouse: "With God all things are possible."

in memory of
David

"The LORD is my light and my salvation—whom shall I fear? The LORD is the stronghold of my life—of whom shall I be afraid?"
Psalm 27:1, NIV

You Can't Take It with You

Here Lies
Solomon, wisest and richest of Israel's kings

THE BODY

When my dad was a toddler, he did something that was quite advanced for his age. His mother was pleased. His grandmother was terrified. She believed a superstition that claimed smart children would die young. About my dad, she said, "He's too smart to live." You can imagine the terrible effect this would have on a child's mother—just waiting for her little boy to die! But he didn't die. In fact, he turned 83 last birthday! He's been pretty smart too.

King Solomon was "too smart to live."

First Kings 3 tells us that, when Solomon became king, God offered him anything he asked. Wow! Can you imagine? Solomon was already smart enough

cause of death

Unknown. His death is mentioned in 2 Chronicles 9:30, 31.

last words

We don't know exactly when each of his proverbs was written. But the book of Ecclesiastes (his term paper on the meaning of life) may have been the last thing he wrote. It ends like this: "Here is my final advice: Honor God and obey his commands. This is the most important thing people can do" (Ecclesiastes 12:13, 14, ICB).

WORDS TO LIVE BY

"Don't store up treasures here on earth. . . . Store your treasures in heaven, where they will never become motheaten or rusty and where they will be safe from thieves."

Matthew 6:19, 20, NLT

DEATH SENTENCE

"I thought success in show business was the answer to everything. It isn't. I don't know what is."

—legendary comedienne Martha Raye (1916–1994)

to ask for the right thing. It would have been so tempting to ask for a whole fleet of cars or $10 million—to be rich and famous. But Solomon asked for wisdom in order to rule the kingdom well.

God was pleased with his request. He gave Solomon wisdom—and, as a bonus, he made Solomon rich and famous. Each year the king received 25 tons of gold, which in today's terms would equal $200 million. He owned 1,400 chariots and 12,000 horses. And much more. He built a grand palace for himself and a glorious temple for the Lord (1 Kings 6, 7, 10). He received gifts from other people who heard of his wisdom and came great distances to consult with him. One such visitor was the Queen of Sheba. When she saw and talked with King Solomon, she said, "In wisdom and wealth you have far exceeded the report I heard" (1 Kings 10:7, NIV).

King Solomon ruled wisely. His reign was a time of incredible prosperity and peace. But in one area he wasn't "too smart to live." He began to

life line —/\/\/\/\/\—

"I've never seen a hearse pulling a U-Haul."

—Charles Swindoll

marry many foreign women. Some of them were probably princesses, daughters brought by foreign kings as part of their gift to King Solomon. Perhaps it would have been nearly impossible to refuse. Multiple wives and political marriages were very common in those days. But the foreign women (of the king's 700 wives and 300 slave girls) brought their religious idols with them. God had warned King Solomon that marrying unbelievers would turn his heart away from God (1 Kings 11). And that's exactly what happened. Solomon allowed places of worship to be built for the false gods. He allowed pagan rituals to take place.

In the end, though, King Solomon was still wise enough to know that following God is the most important thing, that true happiness

of grave concern

It's hard to imagine that all those women wanted to marry King Solomon, considering the things he said to them. In his love poem are these romantic words: "Your hair is like a flock of goats descending from Mount Gilead. Your teeth are like a flock of sheep" (Song of Songs 4:1, 2, NIV).

⟨⟨⟨ EPITAPH ⟩⟩⟩

Seven wives I've buried
With many a fervent
    prayer;
If we all should meet in
    Heaven,
Won't there be trouble
    there?

—unknown

HEART-STOPPER
"You can't have everything. Where would you put it?"

—advice columnist Ann Landers

doesn't come from money or things—
or even other people (see his last
words above).

He wrote most of the book of
Proverbs, which has a chapter for
every day of the month. Try reading a
chapter a day and pick out a bit of
wisdom to follow for that day. You'll
be really smart, God will surely throw in some bonuses and who
knows—you might even live to be 83!

in memory of
Solomon

"The LORD gave Solomon wisdom, just as he had promised him."
1 Kings 5:12, NIV

ALL THE KING'S HORSES

Here Lies
Ahaziah, eighth king of Israel
(there were two Ahaziahs)

THE BODY

When I lived in Japan, I saw all kinds of religious practices. I saw: people ringing bells to wake up the gods, written prayers tied to holy trees, little meals of rice and mandarin oranges set out for the ancestors, coin offerings placed on a cow statue . . . I even saw tiny "horses" outside people's gates, placed there for the spirits of the dead to ride home on for a visit. The horse body was either a cucumber or an eggplant. The legs were pieces of broken chopsticks stuck into the body.

cause of death
He never recovered from falling through the latticework in an upper room of his palace (2 Kings 1:2, 17).

last words
When he was told that someone had predicted his death, he asked for a description of the man. Upon hearing the description, he said, "It was Elijah" (2 Kings 1:8, ICB).

Non-Asian readers might think, *Well, that sounds kind of . . . uh, stupid. How could people believe in stuff like that?* Especially modern people carrying cell phones and riding the Bullet Train.

WORDS TO LIVE BY

"Same people say, 'Ask the mediums and fortune-tellers what to do. They whisper and mutter and ask dead people what to do.' But I tell you that people should ask their God for help. Why should people who are still alive ask something from the dead? You should follow the teachings and the agreement with the Lord. The mediums and fortune-tellers do not speak the word of the Lord. Their words are worth nothing."

Isaiah 8:19, 20, ICB

But, wait a minute. Do you have any friends who call a psychic, carry a crystal, check their horoscope, have their palm read, wear a "lucky" article of clothing or consult a Ouija® talking board? *Oh.*

King Ahaziah knew about the true God. But when he was concerned about his future, he didn't pray to God and place his life in God's hands. He went to a lesser god.

The story in 2 Kings 1 is pretty funny.

Poor King Ahaziah had shattered himself by falling off his palace.

SIX-FEET-DEEP THOUGHT

Pray for the nation
Or your occupation
About a donation
Or your education
Show appreciation
Give thanks for creation
To find consolation
In times of temptation
Seekin' salvation
And soul satisfaction
Hangin' in traction
Group meditation
Sin infestation . . .
You got to pray.

—from the rap "When to Pray" by Jenna Lusby

(That's not the funny part.) Then, instead of praying to God or sending for a real servant of the real God (like Elijah), he sent messengers to consult the false god Baal-Zebub.

God ordered Elijah to intercept them. Elijah sent them back to the king to say that the king would not recover from his injuries—because he had failed to take his concerns to the true God.

When the king realized he was dealing with Elijah, he sent more messengers. (This is the funny part.) But Elijah, instead of coming down to meet them, called down fire from Heaven to destroy them. King Ahaziah kept hearing about dead messengers—and sending more messengers. The third batch of messengers was not at all happy about going! They begged Elijah for mercy, and they were spared.

life line —wwwww

"Our prayers lay down the track on which God's power can come."
—Watchman Nee

⌘ EPITAPH ⌘

Humpty Dumpty sat on
    a wall
Humpty Dumpty had a
    great fall
All the king's horses and
    all the king's men
Couldn't put Humpty
    Dumpty together again.
—the famous
nursery rhyme

HEART-STOPPER

The August 2003 *Reader's Digest* told the story of Justin Kirkbride. His small plane crashed. He was picked up by a rescue helicopter, and it crashed. So the man fell to Earth in two air crashes within 16 hours on the same mountain. He survived.

But the king did die, as the Lord had said.

What would the messengers have found out if they'd made it to the temple of Baal-Zebub? They may have learned the right answer to their question. You may sometimes get a right answer from a psychic or from a cow statue with a coin on its back. But those methods still don't "work" because they're forbidden by God. God gives us the answers we need to know in the Bible. And he personally guides us when we pray to him.

You can consult many sources to find answers to the questions of life, but the best course of action is to take your concerns straight to the one true God. You don't want to end up riding through the air on a cucumber horse.

 ## midnight tale

Second Kings 10 tells how King Jehu wiped out Baal worship in Israel. He pretended that he was going to offer a sacrifice to Baal. He invited all the false prophets of Baal to meet him at a Baal temple. But he destroyed the false prophets, demolished the sacred stone from inside the temple and tore down the temple. The location was then used as a public toilet (v. 27).

in memory of
Ahaziah

"I will surely repay you for your conduct. . . . then you will know that I am the LORD."
Ezekiel 7:4, NIV

✝ CHARIOT OF FIRE

Here Lies

Elijah, the prophet whose name means "My God is Jehovah"

THE BODY

It would have been fun to hear the weather report in Elijah's day:

"... should expect a little snow in the mountain regions by nightfall. The plains will enjoy above-normal temperatures.... And in the area surrounding Elijah—wind, drought, black clouds, earthquakes, heavy rains and an unusual lightning-fire phenomenon ..." Yes, in the area surrounding Elijah it would have been hard to know what to wear to school!

Elijah was God's messenger during the reign of King Ahab. Most of the other kings' Bible accounts are very short. But King Ahab's story takes up all the space from 1 Kings 16–2 Kings 1. That's not because of King Ahab. It's the fabulous story of Elijah.

cause of death

"Unnatural causes." A chariot of fire and horses of fire carried him away alive in a whirlwind to Heaven (2 Kings 2:11).

last words

In answer to Elisha's request to receive a share of Elijah's power: "If you see me when I am taken from you, it will be yours. If you don't, it won't happen" (2 Kings 2:10, ICB).

◌◌◌ EPITAPH ◌◌◌

Now that ain't too bad.
—on a tombstone
in Chicago

The most famous episode in Elijah's life was his showdown on Mt. Carmel against the false prophets of Baal (1 Kings 18). One man of God against hundreds of false prophets. Elijah vs. the notorious King Ahab and Queen Jezebel. One invisible God against visible images of Baal. When you read the story, don't think cartoon; think Spielberg. It's terrifying!

Elijah single-handedly challenged the false prophets to prove the powers of Baal. The true God, he said, would send fire from Heaven to ignite the sacrifice. He gave the false prophets all day to pray to their god. Nothing happened. He got tired of waiting and even began to taunt them—though they could have had him killed at any moment.

Then Elijah took center stage. He even put his God at a disadvantage by watering down the entire altar. He prayed one sentence in total faith: "O Lord, answer me! Answer me so these people will know that you, O Lord, are God" (1 Kings 18:37, NLT). Fire came down and consumed the sacrifice—along with the stones and the water. The people fell on their faces.

life line —〰〰〰

"Now go take on the day."
—Dr. Laura's sign-off words

Doing scary things for God is cool. But it isn't easy. In your early childhood Sunday school class, your teacher probably didn't tell you what came after the Mt. Carmel event. Queen Jezebel, furious at being humiliated, chased after Elijah. Who knows what kind of torture she would have subjected him to had she caught him! Elijah ran as far as he could. Then he sat down all alone. He wanted to die. He cried, "God, I can't take any more" (see 1 Kings 19:4). When you do scary things for God you have to take the bad with the good.

A lot of young adults complain about being bored. You don't *have* to be bored. You can be as fiery as Elijah. Just ask the Lord to show you something important to do for him. Then do it.

Uh, better take a change of clothes. You never know what kind of weather you'll have.

DEATH SENTENCE

*"When I leave, I want to go out like Elijah
With a whirlwind to fuel my chariot of fire
And when I look back on the stars
It'll be like a candlelight in Central Park
And it won't break my heart to say goodbye."*

—from the song "Elijah" by Rich Mullins, © 1982 Meadowgreen Music Company/BMG Songs/ASCAP. All rights administered by EMI CMG Publishing.

HEART-STOPPER

Get in.
Sit down.
Shut up.
Hold on.
—seen on a bumper sticker

"AP Technoglass. Ron speaking."

Ron worked in the guardhouse of the company. Ron had a wonderful deep, commanding, masculine voice. Many places of business around town had occasion to telephone AP Technoglass daily. Lady workers actually fought for the opportunity to be the one to place the call. They wanted to talk to Ron. There was something about his voice.

In Revelation 1:15, the Lord's voice is described as the sound of rushing water. In 1 Kings 19:12, God spoke to Elijah in a gentle whisper. The Lord is speaking to us when we read his words in the Bible. There is something about the Lord's voice.

in memory of
Elijah

"I have zealously served the LORD God Almighty."
1 Kings 19:10, NLT

No One Cried

Here Lies
Jehoram, fifth king of Judah (there were two Jehorams)

THE BODY

In the movie *Trading Places,* Billy Ray Valentine is a young man who has grown up in the ghetto. His behavior is pretty outlandish. Louis Winthorpe III, on the other hand, has been privileged. He's very cultured and is now a wealthy stockbroker. The movie deals with the question: did the two men turn out the way they did simply because of their families? In other words, was it in their genes? Or does everything depend on a person's circumstances? Bad settings produce bad people; good settings produce good people. Louis's old uncles have had an ongoing debate about the topic of nature vs. nurture. They wanted to experiment. So they set up a scheme to bring Billy Ray into

cause of death

Around 840 B.C. "The LORD afflicted Jehoram with an incurable disease of the bowels. In the course of time, at the end of the second year, his bowels came out because of the disease, and he died in great pain." Though he was buried in the city of the kings, he was not buried in the tombs of the kings (2 Chronicles 21:18-20, NIV).

last words

No recorded words.

God "commanded our ancestors to teach [his truths] to their children, so the next generation might know them—even the children not yet born—that they in turn might teach their children. So each generation can set its hope anew on God, remembering his glorious miracles and obeying his commands."

Psalm 78:5-7, NLT

the firm and to toss Louis out on the streets with nothing— just to see how they'll respond.

Circumstances turned out to be more important than genes. Billy Ray adapted to his new surroundings and became an honest and very insightful stockbroker. Poor Louis went nuts—he didn't know how to manage without his money and his butler.

Jehoram came from a good family. He had a good father and a good grandfather—so he had good genes. Then he married the wicked Athaliah who came from a horrible family (her story is coming up)— and put himself in bad circumstances. He adapted to the bad

⟨⟩ EPITAPH ⟨⟩

Here lies the body of Mary
  Ann Lowder;
She burst whilst drinking a
  Seidlitz powder;
Called from this world to
  her heavenly rest,
She should have waited till
  it effervesced.

—in Massachusetts. (A
  Seidlitz powder was a
  mild laxative made of
  two powders that were
  dissolved separately,
  combined and drunk—
  after fizzing . . . tasty!)

circumstances. When he took the throne at age 32, he had his six brothers killed, along with some other nobles of the land. He instituted the pagan religions his wife's family had followed.

Not much more is written about Jehoram, really, except that everyone was glad when he died. Perhaps his life was so horrible, the Bible writers didn't even want to give him the satisfaction of putting it in print.

Sometimes people make excuses for their behavior (or have excuses made for them). A guy goes bad and people say, "After all, he comes from a bad family." A girl goes bad and people say, "It's understandable. She just didn't have the right opportunities."

Billy Ray and Athaliah and Louis and Jehoram . . . There are no excuses. Neither bad genes nor bad circumstances determine your destiny. If you don't have a good

of grave concern

"When I die . . . I want some human being somewhere to weep for me."

—the infamous atheist Madalyn Murray O'Hair. She disappeared in 1995. Her body was found in 2000. She had been murdered, dismembered and burned. There is little evidence that anyone mourned her death.

DEATH SENTENCE

"When he dies, he isn't gunna gu like everybudy else. He's just gunna nasty away."

—Andy, speaking uf cruel businessman Ben Weaver, *the Andy Griffith Shuw*

SIX-FEET-DEEP THOUGHT

In September 2003 one of the tabloids announced that Jerry Springer said, "Midget vampire hookers ruined my career."

life line —〰〰〰

"The evil that men do lives after them."

—Marc Antony, in William Shakespeare's *Julius Caesar*, Act 3, Scene 2

family, you can start your own new family tree by accepting God as your Father. And, if you've been cheated out of opportunities, you can change your circumstances by deciding to live in the will of God.

midnight tale

Even animals respond to their surroundings. A man told about watching the horror movie *Wolf* with his gentle little poodle. In the movie, actor Jack Nicholson ran with a pack of very violent wolves. When the movie was over, the man leaned over to give the poodle a good-night kiss—and the little rascal bit him.

✳

in memory of
Jehoram

"He passed away, to no one's regret."
2 Chronicles 21:20, NIV

ALL DRESSED UP AND NO PLACE TO GO

Here Lies
Jezebel, a most wicked queen

THE BODY

One minute she was fixing her hair and putting on eye makeup (2 Kings 9:30). The next minute (v. 33) Queen Jezebel's blood was splattering on the wall. It gets worse. When they went to bury her, well . . . uh . . . the dogs had already been at the body. All that remained were her skull, hands and feet. Gag!

cause of death
Thrown from her window and run over by King Jehu's chariot (2 Kings 9:33).

last words
Spoken to King Jehu: "Have you come in peace, you murderer?" (2 Kings 9:31, NLT).

What a terrible way to die. But, you see, God will put up with evil for only so long. And that's what Queen Jezebel was: pure evil.

She was first a pagan princess. When Ahab became king of Israel (and he was no saint himself!), he married her, making her the queen over God's people. Bad move. She brought in all the false religions with their wicked ceremonies. Knowledge of the true God may have been lost forever, if it hadn't been for the prophet Elijah's work.

Jezebel sponsored nearly 1,000 prophets of false gods; she killed people to get what she wanted (1 Kings 21:7, 13, 14). When Elijah called down God's fire from Heaven (1 Kings 18)—proving that Jezebel's gods were fake—everyone was scared to death . . . except Jezebel. She went after Elijah. And she swore by the false gods that she'd kill him (1 Kings 19:2). But God didn't let her. Hee, hee.

On this day she had made herself up and sat in her window acting all gorgeous and important. Her husband had died; so maybe, having heard King Jehu was on his way, she planned to flirt with him. Or maybe she was simply feeling powerful. Whatever her motives, maybe God just couldn't take it anymore.

There was a purpose in not having enough left of Jezebel's body for a proper burial. We get a kind of peace by going to the cemetery where our loved ones are buried. We can stand there, where their bodies are, and remember them as they were. But in Jezebel's case, there was so little left, no one would be able to stand at

SiX-FEEᵼ-DEEP ᵼHOUGHᵼ

"For three days after death, hair and fingernails continue to grow but phone calls taper off."

—Johnny Carson

her grave without remembering this gruesome story. They would be thinking, *Here lies the body . . . or at least the feet . . . that is, I guess it's her feet . . .*

No glory, no honor, no peace.

Never mind that Jezebel's body wasn't left behind. She didn't leave anything else behind either. No legacy, nothing good to be remembered for. There are no schools named after her, no hospitals, no scholarships. There's no indication anyone was sorry she died. Her goal seemed to be to wipe out everyone who believed in the true God. But God didn't let her. Hee, hee.

of grave concern

Two wicked ladies made the American Film Institute's Top 10 list of the worst villains in movie history. No. 10 was the wicked queen in *Snow White*. No. 4 was the Wicked Witch of the West in *The Wizard of Oz*.

∽ EPITAPH ∽

Here lie I, and no wonder I
    am dead,
For the wheel of a wagon
    went over my head.
                —in Pembrokeshire,
                England

I guess Jezebel did leave us something after all: She left us a model of how *not* to live.

The next time you're upset because the bad guys seem to be winning, take heart. Bad plans may succeed for a while, but only for a while.

in memory of
Jezebel

"The wicked are crushed by their sins, but the godly have a refuge when they die."
Proverbs 14:32, NLT

✝ Black Widow

Here Lies
Athaliah, queen of Judah

THE BODY

They were racing to make the car ferry. "We can make it!" Judy insisted. Howard didn't think so. The car ferry pulled away from shore. "We can make it!" Judy repeated. Howard didn't think so. Their tiny car sailed off the ramp; and, just before it hit the water, Judy had time to say, "I don't think we can make it." (A scene from the movie *What's Up, Doc?*)

"I think we can make it." Famous last words. Whatever occurs after famous last words is pretty alarming. Other famous last words you may have heard (or said) are:

"Nice doggie."

"I wonder what this extra wire is for."

"That's probably just thunder."

cause of death

The military commanders "seized her as she reached the entrance of the Horse Gate on the palace grounds, and there they put her to death" (2 Chronicles 23:15, NIV).

last words

Athaliah thought she had wiped out all possible contenders for the throne. Upon learning that little Prince Joash had been hidden until he could be installed as the rightful king to replace her, she cried: "Treason! Treason!" (2 Chronicles 23:13, NIV).

SIX-FEET-DEEP THOUGHT

The custom of widows wearing black at a funeral goes back to a superstition. Supposedly, the dead husband's spirit might try to come back and bother the widow. Black would be more difficult for anyone from the spirit world to see.

"What could possibly go wrong?"

"Watch this!"

"Trust me. I know what I'm doing."

Anyone who says those famous last words probably hasn't thought things through carefully. It pays to take a little time and think about the long-term consequences of our actions.

When Athlaliah's husband the king died, her son assumed the throne. Soon he was killed. It doesn't seem like Athaliah was sad over either of those deaths. Instead, Athaliah saw her chance to take over the throne, and she quickly decided to do something about it. "What could possibly go wrong?" she may have said. Famous last words. Athaliah hadn't thought things through. Her plan was flawed.

"Watch this!" was her attitude as she jumped in and had all the male members of the royal household killed. Never mind that they were her family—she focused only on clearing the way. She would have taken out her

EPITAPH

"Ding, dong, the witch is dead."

—sang the Munchkins in the movie *The Wizard of Oz*

own baby grandson too—but he had been hidden safely away.

Athaliah sat as queen for six years. Though we don't have details of her rule, it must have been awful. Athaliah, not being a clear-thinking person, was probably unpredictable. She was exactly the type to say, "Trust me. I know what I'm doing." But her subjects no doubt lived in fear, wondering what she would do next.

When the time came for her to be deposed so the rightful king could take the throne, she spoke her real last words. She thoughtlessly blurted out, "Treason! Treason!" Her irrational screams made no sense; no one had betrayed her. Thanks to some God-fearing people, things were simply being put right again. *She* was the one who had betrayed her whole family.

Athaliah didn't think ahead. She didn't think about her family. She didn't think about God.

"I can make it! I can make it! . . . I don't think I can make it."

of grave concern

Nadia Foldes wanted to die in church. So Dr. Kevorkian ("Dr. Death") helped her kill herself in a church building that was run by "a sympathetic priest." Jehoida the priest charged the military commanders to get Queen Athaliah *away* from the building God inhabited in those days: "Do not kill her here in the Temple of the LORD" (2 Chronicles 23:14, NLT).

∽◦∾

STONE-COLD FACT
The black widow spider is one of the most poisonous in North America. It is shiny black with two reddish or yellowish triangles joined in an hourglass shape on its abdomen. It spins its web in the dark. Males and baby spiders are harmless. But the female, if her web is disturbed, may rush out and bite.

HEART-STOPPER

Queen Victoria was the British monarch until 1901. When Queen Victoria's husband Prince Albert died, she was grief-stricken. She wore black clothes of mourning . . . for the next 40 years.

in memory of
Athaliah

"So all the people of the land rejoiced, and the city
was peaceful because Athaliah had been killed."

2 Chronicles 23:21, NLT

✝ The Watchers

Here Lies
Jehoida, high priest when Athaliah took over the throne

THE BODY

Satan hates babies. Throughout history Satan always seems to be engineering plots to get rid of large numbers of babies. He's always watching . . . lurking.

It all started in Genesis 3:15. That's a verse from God's curse on Satan for tempting Eve. It's the first prediction that God is going to come to Earth as a baby: The "child will crush your head. And you will bite his heel" (ICB). God forecast that Satan would bite Jesus' heel (do some damage) but that Jesus would crush Satan's head (destroy him). I think Satan had it in for babies from that point on.

Remember Pharaoh who ordered all the Hebrew baby boys killed in Moses' day? And that all the pagan religions,

cause of death
Unknown. "Jehoida . . . died when he was 130 years old . . . buried in Jerusalem with the kings . . . because he had done much good in Israel for God" (2 Chronicles 24:15, 16, ICB).

last words
Speaking about Athaliah, he said, "Take her out of the Temple, and kill anyone who tries to rescue her. Do not kill her here in the Temple of the LORD" (2 Chronicles 23:14, NLT).

WORDS TO LIVE BY

"From heaven the
LORD looks down
and sees all mankind;
from his dwelling
place he watches all
who live on earth."

Psalm 33:13, 14, NIV

EPITAPH

"Remember the children
when I'm gone."

—Actress Audrey Hepburn
had been working hard
with UNICEF, fighting
against world hunger.
Among her last words was
this statement that would
have made a good epitaph
for Jehoida.

especially those practiced by the Canaanites, included child sacrifices? Babies were offered on altars and sometimes buried in the foundations of new buildings. Then, when Jesus was born as a baby, King Herod ordered a baby slaughter. And what about abortion today—with over 4,000 babies being aborted every day . . . the numbers are staggering.

Satan is after babies, all right. He usually manages to find people to cooperate with him. Queen Athaliah was one of them.

Queen Athaliah would have killed her own grandson, baby Prince Joash, so she could have the throne. But Jehoida and his wife were watching out for the baby. They boldly rescued him, kept him hidden and raised him until

STONE-COLD FACT

Comedian Bob Hope died in July 2003. His obituary was written by a dead man. Often obituaries of famous people are written while they're still alive so that when they die the obituary can hit the news quickly. Who would expect Bob Hope to reach 100? The news report said they thought it was the first time a subject had outlived the obituary writer.

he was 7 years old. Jehoida dedicated himself to the child.

Jehoida set things up to have Athaliah ousted, and he saw Joash installed as the rightful king. The terrific account is in 2 Chronicles 22, 23.

Joash was considered a good king. But he was a mere child. The power behind him was really Jehoida. The Bible says that, when Jehoida crowned the young king, he also presented him with a copy of God's laws. No doubt, Jehoida taught the young king from God's laws every day. Jehoida was watching out for little King Joash both physically and spiritually.

of grave concern

Jehoida "fed" the words of the Lord to little King Joash. A former emperor of Ethiopia took that idea too far. He used to eat pages of the Bible when he felt ill. One day he felt very ill and decided to eat the complete book of Kings. He died before he finished.

—Max Anders

SIX-FEET-DEEP THOUGHT

"A baby is God's opinion that the world should go on."
—Carl Sandburg

Maybe you don't have a Jehoida who has protected you both physically and spiritually. But even if you've had rough times until now and even if you've been far from God until now, you've been watched over. Someone has

HEART-STOPPER

There is a special cemetery for babies in Japan. Thousands of little *jizo* statues are set up in remembrance. The *jizo* in a sense represents both a kind of Buddha and the spirit of the dead child. Many of the little statues are draped with tiny articles of clothing or hold little toys in their hands. What the tour guides don't tell you is that most of the statues represent babies who have been aborted.

watched over you physically—that's why you're alive. And someone is watching over you spiritually—that's why you're reading this book about God. Your "watchers" may have been people or God—or both.

One thing is certain: you were one baby Satan wasn't allowed to have. Thank God.

 ### midnight tale

KHARTOUM, Sudan—A Sudanese airliner plunged into a hillside while attempting an emergency landing Tuesday, killing 115 people and leaving one survivor—a 3-year-old boy who was found injured but alive amid charred corpses. (*USA Today*, 7/9/03)

in memory of
Jehoida

He taught, counseled and watched over King Joash.

Psalm 32:8

FATAL ATTRACTION

Here Lies
Amaziah, son of King Joash, ninth king of Judah

THE BODY

People used to be able to spell *cemetery*. But some time ago I began to notice the word often misspelled: *cemetary, cematery....* What happened? Well, my idea is the change was due to the influence of Stephen King's *Pet Sematary* (the book in 1983 and the movie in 1989). We saw the title everywhere—in bookstores, on TV...

It's interesting that people didn't go completely with the spelling of the title. But, seeing the title so often may have caused us to incorporate it into our mental spelling files. Little by little our minds began tweaking away from the correct spelling—one letter at a time.

cause of death

He was captured in a battle when he led Judah against Israel, but he was allowed to live 15 more years. Then there was a conspiracy against him. He fled, but was chased down (2 Kings 14:17-20).

last words

His last recorded words are a war challenge to the king of Israel: "Come, meet me face to face" (2 Kings 14:8, NIV).

We are influenced by what we see and hear. Sometimes we don't realize what we are incorporating into our mental files. There's just a little tweaking. That illustrates how Satan operates. Satan's good at tweaking.

King Amaziah didn't start out too badly. He was a pretty decent king. (His story is recorded in 2 Chronicles 25.) The zinger comes in verse 14. He and his troops clobbered the enemy, confiscated their gods and brought them back. King Amaziah set up those gods as his own and worshiped them. Surely not! He started worshiping the gods of the losers? Duh. What kind of sense does that make? It was all downhill after that.

Satan lures people in with something small at first . . . small, attractive, seemingly harmless. King Amaziah just took home a few gods. No big deal. He set them up. What's the harm? Then . . . oh, well, might as well try a prayer or two. Tweaking. To the next thing. And the next . . .

EPITAPH

Here lies one Wood
Enclosed in wood—
One Wood within another.
The outer wood
Is very good—
We cannot praise the other.
—in Maine, died 1837

116

Watch out.

Satan wants you to think it's no big deal to listen to dark music, collect occult paraphernalia, explore psychic phenomena or watch a lot of horror movies.

That's how he tweaks—one letter at a time—until your mental files are all messed up.

Then you're his.

Can you spell *cemetery?*

Can you spell *gotcha?*

SIX-FEET-DEEP THOUGHT

"If called by a panther,
Don't anther."

—Ogden Nash

DEATH SENTENCE

"By the pricking of my thumbs,
Something wicked this way comes."

—second witch in William Shakespeare's *Macbeth*

HEART-STOPPER

Sir Walter Raleigh's last words were: "This is a sharp medicine, but a sure remedy for all evils."

midnight tale

A young man named Rich was caught in the trap of satanism. He was on drugs, he thought of suicide, he performed animal sacrifices, he was sexually active, he had nightmares of Satan telling him that it was too late. It was no picnic. One day Rich's mother gathered all his occult objects and burned them. Later he began living with a young woman. They got married but, naturally, there were many problems in their marriage. Mercifully, the young wife was brought to God. At some point, Rich sensed the Lord pulling on him as well. One day he felt the Lord speaking, "Now is the time." Rich fell to his knees. "I caught hold of Christ's robe that day," he said, "and I will never let go."

in memory of
Amaziah

*"Shall I bow down to a block of wood? . . .
Is not this thing in my right hand a lie?"*
Isaiah 44:19, 20, NIV

✝ DEPTHS OF DARKNESS

Here Lies
Jonah, prophet of God

THE BODY

I'm going to call him Brother Roy. I'd heard that Brother Roy, a kind of street preacher, hangs out at university campuses. *Good for him—trying to help those wild college kids turn to the Lord*, I thought. But . . . one day I saw and heard him preach. Boy, was I embarrassed to be a Christian! He was mean and hateful, calling the young people names and telling them they were going straight to Hell. He was screaming, "Repent!" But he wasn't telling them how; he wasn't telling them he cared about them. I almost got the feeling he was glad they were lost. It bothered me. I think Jesus would be gentler, especially if the people in his audience didn't know any better.

cause of death

Unknown. He certainly had a should-have-died experience inside the great fish. Later he was so angry at God's compassion for the city of Nineveh, he wanted to die.

last words

His last recorded words were spoken during his disapproval of God's compassion toward Nineveh: "I am angry enough to die" (Jonah 4:9, NIV).

EPITAPH

He rocked the boat,
Did Ezra Shank.
These bubbles mark

○

○

○

○

Where Ezra sank.

—anonymous

The prophet Jonah may have had a little bit of Brother Roy in him.

God wanted the wild citizens of Nineveh to have another chance at being saved. But Jonah didn't seem to think they deserved a chance. He didn't want to go there at all. When he finally did go (after his detour inside the fish), he wanted to pronounce their doom, not help them repent.

It's true they were a pretty bad bunch.

Nineveh, Assyria, was located across the Tigris River from what is now Mosul, Iraq. The Assyrians were barbaric and proud warriors. They even piled the skulls of the people they conquered in the town square.

In God's eyes, in spite of the fact that they had a certain kind of success and power, they were weak and spiritually poor. (You know, kind of like some of the students on college campuses.) God said, "Nineveh has more than a hundred and twenty thousand people who

SIX-FEET-DEEP THOUGHT

"When God directs you somewhere, you just go."

—John Wetteland, relief pitcher for the Texas Rangers

cannot tell their right hand from their left" (Jonah 4:11, NIV). He meant they were bumbling around in spiritual darkness.

When Jonah ended up in the darkness of the fish's insides, maybe it was kind of symbolic. The people of Nineveh were in darkness. But Jonah's hard-hearted way of thinking was also "in the dark."

In the end, Jonah did the job, but it doesn't seem like he ever really understood God's heart about the situation. We all have a little bit of Jonah and Brother Roy in us. Something in us that wants people to get what's coming to them. It's a dark part of our nature. But when we care about lost people—no matter how bad they are—and want to help them change, we reflect God's light.

of grave concern

Jesus referred to the story of Jonah as a hint about his own resurrection. "As Jonah was three days and three nights in the belly of a huge fish, so the Son of Man will be three days and three nights in the heart of the earth" (Matthew 12:40, NIV).

life line —〰〰〰

John Newton didn't believe in God. Then, in the middle of a storm at sea, he found himself calling on God to save him. He turned from darkness to light. In the 1760s Newton wrote the song "Amazing Grace" which is, by far, the most frequently played folk hymn at funeral and memorial services.

midnight tale

It may have been a whale shark that swallowed Jonah. The December 1992 *National Geographic* magazine ran an article describing how that would have happened. Jonah, it said, could easily have been sucked into the whale shark's enormous mouth. He would have slid right past the thousands of tiny teeth and down into the large cardiac stomach. Jonah would not have been able to swim back out. Fortunately, he wouldn't have been able to go the other way either! Sensing that this large object would not easily be digested, the whale shark would expel the contents of the cardiac stomach.

in memory of
Jonah

God does not want "anyone to perish,
but everyone to come to repentance."
2 Peter 3:9, NIV

Nightmare!

Here Lies
Sennacherib and the Assyrian army

THE BODY

Archaeologists are still trying to uncover the entire terra cotta army of Emperor Qin. He ruled China from 221-207 B.C. When he was only 13 he ordered the construction of his own tomb. Archaeologists are unearthing it. So far, in three different pits, they have discovered thousands of life-size soldier statues, not to mention many statues of horses and chariots. The soldiers have different faces and appear to be of different ranks—just like a real army. Presumably the army would defend Emperor Qin in the afterlife.

Did he really believe soldiers of clay could protect him?

cause of death

"The angel of the LORD . . . killed 185,000 Assyrian troops" (2 Kings 19:35, NLT). Sennacherib "was worshiping in the temple of his god Nisroch" and his sons "killed him with their swords" (2 Kings 19:37, NLT).

last words

In a message to King Hezekiah of Judah: "Don't let this God you trust deceive you with promises that Jerusalem will not be captured . . ." (2 Kings 19:10, NLT).

123

"Destruction is certain for those who . . . [trust] their cavalry and chariots instead of looking to the LORD. . . . In his wisdom, the LORD will send great disaster."

Isaiah 31:1, 2, NLT

STONE-COLD FACT

The Bible says that the day of the Lord (which is understood to mean the second coming of Jesus) "will come like a thief in the night" (1 Thessalonians 5:2, NIV).

King Sennacherib's headquarters were in the Assyrian capital of Nineveh.

During the reign of a previous king, many people in Nineveh had turned to God as a result of Jonah's visit. Modern tradition even places Jonah's grave there.

But King Sennacherib was not a follower of God. On this particular day, the king and his troops were camped on the outskirts of Jerusalem, gearing up for an attack. Sennacherib had been sending messages to King Hezekiah, threatening to take over Jerusalem. His taunting words to King Hezekiah were very insulting to God: "Don't think you can count on that God of yours . . ."

King Sennacherib was totally confident. He had conquered other nations, backed by his powerful army. The king didn't know it, but he had conquered his last nation, and he had insulted God for the last time.

That night the angel of the Lord

SIX-FEET-DEEP THOUGHT

"Judgment day is inevitable."
—Terminator, *Terminator 3: Rise of the Machines*

swept through the camp (You gotta wonder what *that* sounded like!) and killed 185,000 soldiers. But the death angel passed over the king. The king woke up to the nightmare of finding himself in a field of corpses. He quickly retreated to Nineveh.

What more evidence did King Sennacherib need to prove that God the creator was supreme? But, even after this display of God's power, the king didn't acknowledge him. Later we find him back in his pagan temple, worshiping the false god Nisroch. And there, for some unknown reason, his two sons attacked and killed him.

King Sennacherib had surrounded himself with a vast army of men. Men who were—as all men are—created from dust. Did he really believe soldiers of clay could protect him?

We can thank Sennacherib for his lesson about where our real protection comes from.

of grave concern

I heard a fly buzz when I
    died;
The stillness round my
    form
Was like the stillness in the
    air—
Between the heaves of
    storm.
. . . .
With blue, uncertain,
    stumbling buzz,
Between the light and me;
And then the windows
    failed, and then
I could not see to see.

—Emily Dickinson,
"I Heard a Fly Buzz"

EPITAPH

Reader, death took me
    without any warning.
I was well at night and
    dead in the morning.

—unknown

midnight tale

In 1978, the British army temporarily took over for the firemen, who were on strike. An elderly lady called the army to rescue her cat that was stuck up a tree. She was so grateful that, afterward, she invited them all in for tea. As they drove away, they ran over the cat and killed it.

in memory of
Sennacherib and the Assyrian army

"Drained of power . . . and put in shame."
2 Kings 19:26, niv

✝ Cheating Death

Here Lies
Daniel, captive in Babylon and prophet of God

THE BODY

In Europe today, there are supposedly some very macabre memorials: a cathedral chandelier made of bones; burial containers decorated with bones of people; carvings of skeletons in a church . . .

They are reminders of the bubonic plague: the Black Death, a horrifying disease spread by flea-infested rats. In 14th century Europe, death was everywhere. The disease could not be stopped because no one could figure out what was causing it. In the end, half the population of London died. A full one-third of the population of Europe died: 25 million people.

What must it have been like for the survivors who cheated death? How frightening it would be to watch as one out of every three people around you died. Panic. *Surely I'll be next*, they must have thought.

cause of death
Unknown.

last words
His last recorded words were spoken after the Lord showed him a vision of the end times. Daniel asked: "My lord, what will the outcome of all this be?"
(Daniel 12:8, NIV).

life line —〰〰〰
"I refuse to tiptoe through life only to arrive safely at death."

—seen on a T-shirt

Daniel cheated two different kinds of death: physical and spiritual.

Daniel was a young Jewish man when Babylon conquered Jerusalem. He was among the first group of captives taken from Jerusalem to Babylon in 605 B.C. and he was one of several choice young people selected to serve the king of Babylon. In the first place, Daniel could have been killed when Babylon laid siege to Jerusalem. Then, he was in Babylon for almost the rest of his life—during the reign of several different kings. Any of those could have tired of him at any time. And, of course, there was the little matter of being thrown into the lions' den. Daniel was always in physical danger. *Surely I'll be next,* he must have thought on more than one occasion.

Daniel was also in danger of spiritual death. As a young man brought into Babylon, he was to be taught Babylonian ways (Daniel 1:4). The idea was to break down his old beliefs and replace them with Babylonian culture and religious beliefs.

EPITAPH

He has gone from the earth
With its pain and care
He is safe in a realm
That is bright and fair.

—on the tombstone of a 14-year-old boy, Williamstown, Kentucky

128

I don't know how the survivors of the Black Death held on. But I know how Daniel did!

SIX-FEET-DEEP THOUGHT

We walked within the churchyard bounds,
  My little boy and I;
He laughing, running happy rounds,
  I pacing mournfully.

"Nay, child, it is not well," I said,
  "Among the graves to shout,
To laugh and play among the dead,
  And make this noisy rout."

A moment to my side he clung,
  Leaving his merry play;
A moment stilled his joyous tongue,
  Almost as hushed as they.

Then quick, forgetting the command
  In life's exulting burst
Of early glee, let go my hand,
  Joyous as at the first.

. . . .

A triumph won o'er sin and death,
  From these the Saviour saves;
And, like a happy infant, Faith
  Can play among the graves.
  —"A Walk in a Churchyard" by Archbishop Trench, born 1807

HEART-STOPPER

Fear knocked at my door.
Faith answered.
No one was there.

       —unknown

Daniel's deep faith in God never wavered. It gave him an unbelievable calm. In Daniel 2, an enraged King Nebuchadnezzar was going to have Daniel and his friends killed. Most of us would have started screaming or looking for a place to hide. Panic. But verse 15 pictures a calm Daniel merely asking, "Why did the king order such a terrible punishment?" (ICB).

Even though death was always near, Daniel maintained that calm faith by staying close to God. How did he know the Lord was constantly with him? Daniel 6:10 tells us that Daniel always prayed three times a day—even when such prayer was forbidden. That was his secret.

So, when life seems to be falling apart all around you, when "death" is everywhere—remember this: Walking with God daily is the only way to stay dead calm. It worked for Daniel.

in memory of
Daniel

The Lord said, "Remain faithful even when facing death, and I will give you the crown of life."
Revelation 2:10, NLT

✝ IF LOOKS COULD KILL

Here Lies
Esther, the Jewish girl Hadassah who became queen of Persia

THE BODY

There wasn't time to think.

Thick fog had caused an expressway pileup. One truck was already on fire when the women's rugby team from a Pennsylvania university happened on the scene. Their first impulse was to exit their cars and find shelter from the sure-to-explode gas tanks. Then they noticed that other cars were headed full speed toward the wreckage. Two of the young women stood in the middle of flying glass, metal and tire pieces and flagged drivers.

cause of death
Unknown.

last words
Her last recorded words are in Esther 9:13. But her most famous words—what she thought would be her last words— are in Esther 4:16. She took her life in her hands to approach the king uninvited and said: "I will go to the king. . . . And if I perish, I perish" (NIV).

Other cars were beginning to blaze. Victims were screaming. The other team members started helping people, using what first aid they knew.

Three hours later the rugby team had done all they could. They huddled to pray for the victims. In all there had been four people killed and 37 injured in the 28-car pileup.

Officer Stackhouse said of the young women: "They placed themselves in danger when others just sat in their cars."

Esther didn't have time to think. It was probably just as well.

The beautiful Jewish girl was suddenly whisked away to the palace of King Xerxes of Persia who was looking for a new queen. He had tossed the old one when she refused to attend his drunken party. All the beautiful girls being considered were given a year's worth of beauty treatments. Then King Xerxes slept with them to choose a favorite as queen. He chose Esther. But he didn't know she was Jewish.

There wasn't much Esther could do about her situation except to behave wisely—which she did.

Esther *did* have time to think when she faced the crisis she is best known for.

King Xerxes had been convinced that he needed to rid his nation of all

SIX-FEET-DEEP THOUGHT
What happens if you get scared "half to death" twice?
—unknown

the Jewish people residing there. Esther's cousin Mordecai sent word to Esther, challenging her to speak to the king on behalf of the Jewish people. Esther 4 shows us Esther's thought process—she well knew the danger she would be in. Being the queen gave her no real power. It would be presumptuous—unheard of—to approach the king uninvited. And what would happen when the king found out that Esther herself was Jewish? That could make matters even worse.

Esther made the choice to place herself in danger to save others. And she succeeded.

Both the rugby ladies and Esther could have been killed for their trouble. But some things are worth the risk.

Anything facing you that scares you to death? You feel God nudging you to take the risk? Take another look at Esther, then go for it!

 **midnight tale**

The movie *Schlindler's List* is about a man who helped save Jewish people from the Holocaust. At the end of the movie, there is a parade of the real survivors of the Holocaust, along with their children, traveling to pay their respects at Schindler's grave. Those survivors and all their descendants ever after owe their lives to him. Esther saved the Jewish people from extinction at the hand of King Xerxes. It was a truly significant event when you consider that Jesus was among the later descendants of the Jews.

in memory of
Esther

She pleased the king of Persia and the king of Heaven.
Esther 9:13

REMEMBER ME

Here Lies
Nehemiah, cupbearer to the king of Persia and governor of the Jews

THE BODY

Steve was being bullied. When he finally got up the nerve to tell a teacher, the teacher advised him to find the bully's weakness. Steve asked around and learned that the bully never rode the rides at the amusement park—he was afraid of heights. One day the bully took Steve's lunch and dared him to meet outside to fight for it. Steve stood up in the cafeteria and said for all to hear: "Meet me after school on the roof of the gym." One hundred students gathered to watch. But the bully never showed—and he never messed with Steve again.

Nehemiah knew all about bullies.

First, a little background: Nehemiah's home was Jerusalem, but he was one of many captive Jews in Persia. He impressed the powers-that-be and was given the position of cupbearer—a position I'm not

cause of death
Time, cause and place of death are unknown.

last words
His last recorded words are in Nehemiah 13:31: "Remember me with favor, O my God" (NIV).

135

"We prayed to our God and posted a guard day and night. . . . The surrounding nations were afraid and lost their self-confidence, because they realized that this work had been done with the help of our God."

Nehemiah 4:9; 6:16, NIV

STONE-COLD FACT
There are 12 prayers in the book of Nehemiah, including the longest prayer in the Bible: Nehemiah 9:5-37.

sure I would have wanted. The job of the cupbearer was to taste the king's food and drink for poison! Nehemiah was informed of the terrible conditions back in Jerusalem. When he went to see for himself, he broke down and cried. He developed a plan for rebuilding the city wall and he persuaded King Artaxerxes to appoint him as governor of the Jews and allow him to return to Jerusalem to rebuild the city wall.

Enter the bullies.

Sanballat and Tobiah were leaders of non-Jewish tribes in the region. No doubt they feared that, with the city being rebuilt, the Jews might become powerful and maybe a threat to them. Nehemiah 4 and 6 outline the rebuilding of the wall—and the bullying.

Sanballat taunted the Jews with statements like: "Look at those weak Jews. Can they bring that pile of rubble back to life?"

Tobiah threw in his two cents' worth: "Why, what they're building will fall back down if even a little fox steps on it."

EPITAPH
Gone but not forgotten.
—on many old tombstones

Nehemiah pressed on and the work continued.

Now Sanballat and Tobiah were really mad. Nehemiah had to take half the workers away from the job to stand guard against potential attack.

Well, the wall was finished in a miraculous 52 days (6:15).

What I really like in the story is that Nehemiah knew the bullies' weakness: he knew they didn't have God. Nehemiah kept reminding his workers that God was with them and would help them.

The word *remember* appears often in the book of Nehemiah. Nehemiah reminds his workers to remember God. He asks God to remember the bullies and do something about them. And he often says, "Remember me, O God." I imagine him whispering it. Nehemiah was a strong, wonderful man. But he also was only human. He had to have been afraid of the bullies. So he constantly called on the Lord: "Don't forget about me. I'm still here—you know, doing your work. Remember me."

The bullies never had a chance.

of grave concern

One survey showed that ten percent of people who pray daily don't believe in God.

HEART-STOPPER

"When your knees are knocking, kneel on them."
—seen on a church sign

life line

Some varieties of opossum play dead when they're in danger—that's the origin of the term "playing possum." Some ducks, rodents, reptiles, amphibians . . . and people (!) also play possum when they're in danger.

in memory of
Nehemiah

"A righteous man will be remembered forever."
Psalm 112:6, NIV

When Demons Speak

Here Lies
The homeless man of Gadara

THE BODY

There had never been a movie about demon possession like *The Exorcist.* Thousands of 1973 moviegoers ran straight home from the theaters and called their ministers . . . scared to death. People sat around discussing all the disturbing phenomena relating to the 12-year-old possessed girl: how she was thrown across the room, how she spoke in a creepy voice and, of course, how her head spun completely around.

I watched the movie again when I was much older. This time I didn't focus on the girl. I focused on the young priest who tried to help the girl. He failed. His faith was weak; he had too many doubts about God.

Demons have no doubts about God. James 2:19 is loud and clear about that: "You believe there is one God. Good! Even the

cause of death
Unknown.

last words
His last recorded words are not quoted. But we're told in Luke 8:38, 39 that he wanted to go with Jesus. Jesus, though, wanted him to witness to the people in that area. So he went around town telling what Jesus had done for him.

❦❦❦❦❦❦❦❦❦

WORDS TO LIVE BY

"The smoke of their
torment rises forever
and ever, and they will
have no relief day or
night, for they have
worshiped the beast."

Revelation 14:11, NLT
❦❦❦❦❦❦❦❦❦

demons believe that—and shudder" (NIV). The demons believe, all right. But it's too late for them.

He lived in the cemetery.

Naked.

Around the clock he cried out.

He cut himself.

That's how you end up when you let Satan in: homeless, humiliated, heartbroken and hurting.

We don't know how the homeless man of Gadara became possessed by a demon. Maybe he dabbled in white magic. Maybe he attended séances.

"Oh, come on, aren't those things harmless?" you say. That's probably what *he* thought.

The demons operate on Satan's power—and he *does* have power.

HEART-STOPPER

Students at the Christian campus house of a major university were having a party. They'd invited everybody, including a young couple who happened to be witches. The witches hadn't understood that it was a Christian gathering. They arrived, with the young wife carrying their baby. They soon realized this party was not quite their sort of gig. Just then, one of the Christians popped out from the kitchen and welcomed them with a "Praise Jesus!" Upon hearing the name of Jesus, the wife was so startled she dropped the baby! Her husband helped her pick up the baby (it was fine). Then he said to her: "Don't worry, honey. They didn't ask him to do anything; they only said his name."

Demons know who has the real power, who has the last word. Look at all the hints of it in the story of this homeless man (Mark 5:1-20): The demons fell down at Jesus' feet. They acknowledged him as the "Son of the Most High God." They knew he had the power to do whatever he wanted, and they begged him, "Please don't torture us!" They begged again. They asked him to let them possess a herd of pigs (presumably that was better than being sent back to Hell).

Are you thinking what I'm thinking? They're pathetic!

Stay away from Satan and his demons. Their power is a trap. And anyway, it only lasts until Jesus comes to town.

of grave concern

A missionary to Ethiopia said that when you drive in Ethiopia you see little old ladies, bent over, beside the road. When your car is almost to them, they suddenly dart right in front of it, barely making it across. That's their intention. They believe demons are pursuing them, are on their backs. Their hope is that the car will miss them but hit the demons.

 midnight tale

"Will you walk into my parlor?" said the spider to the fly—

"'Tis the prettiest little parlor that ever you did spy.

The way into my parlor is up a winding stair;

And I have many curious things to show you when you're there."

"Oh, no, no," said the little fly; "to ask me is in vain;

For who goes up your winding stair can ne'er come down again."

Said the cunning spider to the fly—"Dear friend, what can I do

To prove the warm affection I've always felt for you?"

"I thank you, gentle sir," she said, "for what you're pleased to say,

And bidding you good-morning now, I'll call another day."

The spider turned him round about, and went into his den,

For well he knew the silly fly would soon come back again.

. . . .

Alas! Alas! How very soon this silly little fly,

Hearing his wily, flattering words, came slowly flitting by.

. . . .

He dragged her up his winding stair, into his dismal den,

Within his little parlor—but she ne'er came out again!

—from "The Spider and the Fly" by Mary Howitt

in memory of
The homeless man of Gadara

*"God made us free from the power of darkness,
and he brought us into the kingdom of his dear Son."*
Colossians 1:13, ICB

✝ OFF WITH HIS HEAD!

Here Lies
John the Baptist, who prepared the way for Jesus

THE BODY

It's not easy playing second fiddle. I know.

At church camp every year, one girl was awarded an Honor Camper certificate which would entitle her to attend camp free the next year. I came in second—several years in a row. There was no award for that.

When two cheerleaders were chosen from the sixth grade, I came in third. The next year three cheerleaders were chosen from the seventh grade. I came in fourth.

In high school, during tryouts for both the junior and senior plays, I came in second for the lead. That meant I had to be the lead's understudy, learning her

cause of death

Beheading, because he condemned an illicit relationship between King Herod Antipas and his brother's wife (Mark 6:17-29).

last words

We have several testimonies about Jesus that John the Baptist gave, including this one that may contain some of his last words: "Whoever believes in the Son has eternal life, but whoever rejects the Son will not see life, for God's wrath remains on him" (John 3:36, NIV).

part in case she got sick at the last minute. So in order to be prepared for that, I could only have a tiny part in the plays.

John the Baptist was destined to play second fiddle.

The angel Gabriel appeared to Zechariah and Elizabeth to tell them they would have a son. Friends who heard of the miraculous happenings surrounding the child's birth asked, "What then is this child going to be?" (Luke 1:66, NIV). And Zechariah, in a song of praise, sang: "You, my child, will be called a prophet of the Most High; for you will go on before the Lord to prepare the way for him" (Luke 1:76, NIV).

John the Baptist's parents must have raised him in the knowledge that his job would be playing second fiddle to Jesus. I don't find any evidence that John had a problem with that.

I didn't accept my second-fiddle roles as well. I tried to smile and do the whole good sport thing. But inside I was screaming, "When is it going to be *my* turn?" "When do *I* get to be first?"

I didn't understand what John the Baptist understood. The world will slot us into first place, second place, etc. And, when we don't make first place, we feel we've failed. Sometimes we feel we've been cheated out of our spot. But the Lord doesn't measure things the same way. When we do the job he gives us, in the best way we can, even if we're second fiddle to the world, we're No. 1 on his charts.

∞∞ **EPITAPH** ∞∞

Gone, oh gone, our
  brother
So young, so good, so true
Our yearning hearts will
  find another
Oh no! There's none but
  you.

—in Williamstown,
Kentucky, 1847–1876

life line —/\/\/\/\/\—

Another second fiddle in the Bible was Jonathan, son of King Saul. Jonathan would have been the logical heir to the throne. But he knew the Lord had chosen David as the next king. Rather than be jealous of David, Jonathan became David's best friend. He even gave David some of his own royal clothing and armor. Though King Saul often threatened David's life (and even Jonathan's!), Jonathan's loyalty to the king-elect remained strong. The story of this great friendship is told in 1 Samuel.

midnight tale

The legendary comedy duo, George Burns and Gracie Allen, also had a legendary marriage. George reached a higher level of fame than Gracie, partly because Gracie died in 1964 and George lived until 1996—so he had longer to be in the spotlight. But he always considered Gracie to be the better half. His body is said to be buried in a crypt beneath Gracie's—George wanted to make sure she would always have top billing.

in memory of
John the Baptist

Jesus said: "Of all who have ever lived, none is greater."
Matthew 11:11, NLT

✞ Tomb with a View

Here Lies
Lazarus, a good friend of Jesus

✞ THE BODY

"Lord, the one you love is very sick" (John 11:3, NLT). That's the message Mary and Martha sent to Jesus about their brother Lazarus. They were all good friends. Jesus had visited in their home. They were close.

By the time Jesus arrived, Lazarus was dead and buried.

Jesus asked for the stone to be moved away from the tomb. Martha tried to stop him, because Lazarus had been dead four days. "There will be a bad odor," she said. (When my sister and I were kids, we giggled when this part was read from the old *King James Version* of the Bible. It said, "by this time he stinketh" (John 11:39).

cause of death

First time—Illness. Second time— Unknown. We know that the chief priests planned to kill him (John 12:10, 11) because his resurrection drew people to Jesus. Perhaps, at some point, the priests succeeded.

last words

No words of Lazarus are recorded in Scripture. But wouldn't it have been funny if—the second time he died—he had said, "I'm dying . . . and this time I really mean it!"

The four days part is interesting. The Jews had a superstition that a person's soul hung around the body for three days, hoping to return. Since Lazarus had been gone four days, even people who believed that superstition would admit, "That guy's dead."

Then Jesus shouted with confident power, "Lazarus, come out!" And he did.

So, does Jesus raise people from the dead today? Well . . .

Judy's friends were praying for her. ("Lord, one you love is sick.") Judy had a rare disease called Disseminated Intervascular Coagulation (DIC), a complication of cancer treatment. Some doctors say DIC really stands for Death Is Coming because almost all the patients die. Judy was dying. She'd been moved to hospice. Hospice workers deal with dying people all the time. They can chart the symptoms of approaching death. They expected Judy to die in the next few days. Then . . .

A nurse examined Judy. She paused. She looked deep into Judy's eyes and said, "You'd better prepare yourself for a shock. I think you're getting better." ("Judy, come back!")

And Judy, almost Lazarus-like, came back from the grave, as it were. Boy, was the funeral home surprised when she called to cancel her funeral! True story.

Lazarus was extremely close to Jesus. After he "died," he was still close to Jesus. John 12 tells us that the family held a party for Jesus; Lazarus was sitting with him.

Judy was close to Jesus. After she "came back from the dead," she was still close to Jesus. Just a few months after her recovery, she and her artificial leg and Jesus went flying off to Bosnia on a mission trip.

Would you be scared to come back from the dead, knowing you'd have to go through death again? It's kind of the wrong question. The point is to stick close to Jesus all the time so the death part is no big deal.

in memory of
Lazarus

"I am close to God, and that is good.
The Lord God is my protection."

Psalm 73:28, ICB

ZOMBIES

Here Lies
The Pharisees, the religious leaders of Jesus' day

THE BODY

She looked dead, but she wasn't.

Eighty-seven-year-old Carrie Stringfellow was taken from her home to a funeral home, because she "appeared to be dead." (Well, that's what it said in the newspaper.)

The mortician was starting to prepare her body for burial when he heard her mumble something.

Was *he* ever surprised!

In Jesus' time, the Pharisees had the opposite problem of Ms. Stringfellow: they looked alive, but they weren't.

Jesus said they were like nicely painted tombs. They looked good on the out-

cause of death

The Pharisees' rule spanned many years. We can't go into their individual causes of death. But the cause of their spiritual death was their rejection of Jesus.

last words

Their last recorded words are in Acts 23:9. But the last recorded words about Jesus occur at Jesus' death. They said, "His disciples may come and steal the body, and tell the people that he has been raised from the dead . . ." (Matthew 27:64, NIV).

STONE-COLD FACT
"All men die, but not all men really live."
—Mel Gibson as
William Wallace, in
the movie *Braveheart*

side, but inside they were full of dead bones and decay (Matthew 23:27). He meant spiritually. The Pharisees were like spiritual zombies. They were walking around, with the appearance of spiritual life—because they knew God's laws and acted religious—but they were spiritually dead.

The Pharisees were in charge of worship, prayer and sacrifices. Technically, they should have been good ministers. But they added so many of their own extra ideas and rules that a person could barely move without "sinning." They were rigid watchdogs, pretending to be perfect and making everybody else miserable by looking for their mistakes. The Pharisees themselves tried to keep all the rules—or at least put on a good show. For example, some Pharisees tried hard to avoid seeing anything impure or tempting. So they walked around with their eyes closed—and crashed into things. Hard to believe, huh? At any given time, there were a number of Pharisees with bandaged heads.

The Pharisees had the potential to influence many people. But they weren't a positive influence. They were bad witnesses because they

SIX-FEET-DEEP
THOUGHT

Be born once; die twice—
Be born twice; die once.
—unknown

made God look bad. They made following him a burden. Jesus knew that following God should be a joy, not a burden. Jesus was starting to lead people in that different direction; and the Pharisees didn't like him horning in on their territory. They had several clashes.

Jesus couldn't stand the Pharisees' lifestyle. Christ was gentle with people who didn't know any better. But the Pharisees knew better. Some of Jesus' harshest words are directed at them. Matthew 23 lists the Seven Woes of the Pharisees, seven things Jesus said they were messed up on. Their example, instead of drawing people to God, kept them away. They were picky about tithing every little thing, but they didn't really understand love—and they certainly didn't act like it! The Pharisees were hypocrites, perfect examples of how *not* to live.

It would be a good thing to study the lives of the Pharisees, you know, so you don't end up becoming like them. You don't want that—we'd have to take you to the funeral home.

ᙨᕋᕘ **EPITAPH** ᙨᕋᕘ

Go tell the church that I
   am dead
But they need shed no
   tears;
For though I'm dead, I'm
   no more dead
Than they have been for
   years.
—on a minister's tombstone

life line —᙮᙮᙮᙮᙮
"Get an afterlife."
   —on movie posters for *Casper*

midnight tale

Back in the Old Testament, Ezekiel 37 gives us the startling vision of the Valley of Dry Bones. In this vision Ezekiel sees a field of skeletal remains—definitely beyond all hope. Then the bones rise up and are reanimated into a vast army. The nation of Israel had rejected God and had been divided as a people. The vision showed that God could restore them and could fill them with his Spirit.

in memory of
The Pharisees

"Dry bones, hear the word of the LORD!"
Ezekiel 37:4, NIV

DEAD WRONG

Here Lies
Judas Iscariot, who betrayed the Lord

THE BODY

It's an old joke, but . . . One Sunday, a little girl was given two quarters as she left for church—one quarter for the offering and one for herself. As she walked to Sunday school, playing with the quarters in her hand, she dropped one. It rolled through the sewer grate. The girl looked down sadly and said, "There goes God's quarter."

I think most of us have the little girl's attitude. We love money. Money is seductive. We want more and more of it. But people who feed that attitude come to the point where they will do anything to get money. Anything.

cause of death
Suddenly stricken with the reality that he had betrayed Jesus, he hung himself (Matthew 27:5). Acts 1:18 adds that his body fell and burst open.

last words
His last recorded words are: "I have betrayed innocent blood" (Matthew 27:4, NIV).

First Timothy 6:10 says, "The love of money causes all kinds of evil. Some people have left the true faith because they want to get more and more money. But they have caused themselves much sorrow" (ICB).

That's Judas Iscariot in a nutshell.

Judas was one of Jesus' inner circle of 12 apostles. Now, you have to understand that the 12 were mistaken about Jesus' mission. All the Jews were expecting the Messiah. They thought he would be an earthly king. Rome was occupying their country. They were terribly oppressed. They hoped the Messiah would overthrow Rome, giving the Jews both power and peace.

One by one, as the 12 apostles joined with Jesus, they were attracted to his message of hope. But they still thought he would be initiating political change—not just changing people's hearts. They wanted to be at his side, to help restore their country.

In the case of Judas, I think he was hoping for personal power and wealth. John 12:6 tells us that he carried the money bag for the apostles, and John whispers to us that Judas used to "help himself" to the money.

Then he betrayed Jesus. Dropped him right into the hands of the enemy—for a few measly bucks (Matthew 26:15).

Judas probably joined with Jesus in the first place because he thought Jesus was on his way to becoming a megastar who would bring in lots of cash. While Judas waited, he volunteered to carry the apostles' money bag so he could sneak money from it. I can't help thinking that perhaps Judas always was scheming ways to get money. Maybe money was Judas's whole purpose in life. People like that develop a very cold heart.

I wonder if Judas got to the point where he felt things weren't moving fast enough. It was taking too long for Jesus to become king. Judas wanted money now. So when the chief priests offered him 30 coins to hand Jesus over, it seemed like a good opportunity. Just business.

The story ends quickly and badly. Reality hit Judas smack in the face, and he tried to undo the damage. He tried to cancel the deal, give the money back. The chief priests wouldn't take the money. Judas threw it at them. Then he hung himself.

of grave concern

The 30 coins Judas received in exchange for Jesus were probably large shekels called tetradrachms . . . worth about 75 cents each.

DEATH
SENTENCE

"Money can control you—whether you have any or not—because if you think money is the answer to all your problems, then money is your god."

—Clint Pratt

⟜ EPITAPH ⟜

Here lies John Hill
A man of skill
His age was five times ten.
He ne'er did good
Nor ever would
Had he lived as long again.

—unknown

If you ever drop one of your quarters in the sewer, take a good look at the one left in your hand. And think of Judas.

 ## midnight tale

Remember the story of the poor widow in the Bible who gave her last coins as an offering to God (Mark 12:41-44)? Someone estimated that if her money had been deposited in the First National Bank of Jerusalem, drawing interest of four percent compounded semi-annually, the fund today would amount to $4,800,000,000,000,000,000,000. So, should she have banked it? No. First, she would have been dead long before the money amounted to anything. And second, she did the right thing. We have to trust God, not people, for financial help. The best way for that widow to have her needs met was to give those last coins to God—not put them in the bank or even buy a sandwich with them. The widow was smart enough to know that only God could fix her situation. I just know something great happened to her when she left that temple. If a mere bank could multiply a couple of coins to an astronomical figure, think how God, the all-powerful creator, is able to multiply whatever we give him!

in memory of
Judas Iscariot

"It would be better for him if he had not been born."
Mark 14:21, NIV

✝ Living Will

Here Lies
Mary, mother of Jesus of Nazareth

THE BODY

Millions of people visit her shrines—at Lourdes in France, Fatima in Portugal and Our Lady of Guadalupe in Mexico. Some villagers say she appears to them regularly at Medjugorje in Bosnia-Herzegovina, and millions have made the pilgrimage to that site. There are stories of weeping statues and bleeding statues. Many people call her the Mother of God and the Queen of Heaven.

She's dead. But if she knows what's going on here on Earth, I have a feeling she doesn't like all that attention going to her.

Let's do a little investigating into the life of Mary, the mother of Jesus.

cause of death
Unknown.

last words
Though she lived at least some years beyond the incident, her last recorded words took place at Jesus' first miracle, the turning of the water into wine. Mary told the servants: "Do whatever [Jesus] tells you" (John 2:5, NIV).

She makes very few appearances in the Bible. And, during most of those, she doesn't speak. There was the time the angel told her of Jesus' birth; the actual birth of Jesus and events surrounding that; with Jesus at age 12; at the first miracle in Cana; an instance or two of her trying to get to Jesus when he was ministering to people; she was present at the cross when Jesus died; and the last appearance is after Jesus has risen and ascended to Heaven. At that time, she is with all the apostles in a prayer meeting (Acts 1:14).

Mary spoke some key words that give us insight into her character. When the angel Gabriel explained everything that would happen regarding the birth of Jesus, she responded: "I am the Lord's servant, and I am willing to accept whatever he wants. May everything you have said come true" (Luke 1:38, NLT). And her last words, "Do whatever he tells you," have the same heart.

Notice the *whatever*s. Whatever God wants. Whatever Jesus says.

Mary was a young woman who simply wanted to live in the will of God. Whatever God wanted. It wasn't about her. It was about God.

EPITAPH

Her task in life, divinely planned,
Was finished with the fading light;
She took her ready lamp in hand
And softly said, "Goodnight."

—in Bridgton, Maine, died 1912

160

How can you live in the will of God?

WANT IT.

"Lord, tell me your ways. Show me how to live. Guide me in your truth. Teach me, my God, my Savior. I trust you all day long" (Psalm 25:4, 5, ICB).

LEARN IT

"Using the Scriptures, the person who serves God will be ready and will have everything he needs to do every good work" (2 Timothy 3:17, ICB).

DO IT.

"Not everyone who says to me, 'Lord, Lord,' will enter the kingdom of heaven, but only he who does the will of my Father who is in heaven" (Matthew 7:21, NIV).

Make God's will the focus of your life, as Mary did. If Mary could see what's going on here on Earth . . . she'd love it.

 midnight tale

Famous dramatic actress Joan Crawford's image was shattered with the release of the notorious book *Mommy Dearest*. In the book, Joan's daughter outlined a childhood filled with abusive treatment by her mother. Joan Crawford then revised her will to include this statement: "It is my intention to make no provision herein for my son . . . or my daughter . . . for reasons which are well known to them."

in memory of
Mary

"I am not important, but God has shown his care for me, his servant girl."
Luke 1:48, ICB

✝ Drop Dead

Here Lies
Ananias and Sapphira, members of the church in Jerusalem

THE BODY

I would have to lie. I had no choice.

We had come back to the U.S. after ten years in Japan. We needed a place to live. But we had no job; we had nothing but a suitcase each. And, because we had been living overseas, there was no way for anyone to call up the telephone company or the electric company to see if we were honest people who paid bills on time. We didn't even have U.S. driver's licenses. We looked very suspicious.

Already we'd hit several dead-ends in our search for housing. Apartment managers wouldn't even consider us because we had more than the limit of two children. One horrible little house was available to rent; but the ceiling was so low

cause of death

Having been caught in their lie, Ananias dropped dead. Three hours later, Peter said to Sapphira, "The feet of the men who buried your husband are at the door, and they will carry you out also" (Acts 5:9, NIV). At that moment she dropped dead.

last words

Ananias—No words. Sapphira—Peter asked, "Is this the price you and Ananias got for the land?" Her last words were a lie: "Yes," she said, "that is the price" (Acts 5:8, NIV).

my husband would have had to walk bent over all the time. *Please, God, don't make us live there!*

Then we spotted it. A three-bedroom brick home in the nicest area of town: For Sale or Rent. I called and learned that the rent was no more than for the low-ceilinged shack. Hmm. I made an appointment to see the house.

That's when I decided to tell the absolute truth. Hadn't I just been praying for God to help us? Since the Lord *is* truth (John 14:6), how could he help if I lied?

The house was everything we needed and more. But my conversation with the owner was pretty funny:

Owner: But your husband *does* have a job?

Me: Not really. The mission will pay our salary two more months, then . . .

HEART-STOPPER

In a list of Silly Government Proposals, the August 2003 *Reader's Digest* included this one: "The mayor of Mount Sterling, Iowa, tried to ban lying. Honest."

Owner: But you own a home here already?

Me: Oh, no. We're just camped out at my sister's.

Owner: Well, have you ever been refused credit?

Me: Oh, everywhere we go! We've been out of the country for ten years. There's really no paperwork on us here.

The owner's realtor friend was beginning to twitch and signal NO to the owner. The owner asked all his questions, and I had no good answers. We stood facing each other in dead silence. *It's over,* I thought.

Suddenly the owner threw back his head, slapped his leg and laughed loudly. "Doggone it," he said, "I like you!"

And that's how we got the house in the nicest part of town—with the swimming pool.

Ananias and Sapphira didn't have to lie.

The story is found in Acts 5. The church people were putting all their possessions into a common fund to share equally. But it

of grave concern

A woman discovered that her husband had been cheating on her. She was so upset—she considered both murder and suicide. Deciding to kill herself, she leaped blindly out her third-floor window. But she survived. Something had broken her fall. She had landed on top of her husband . . . killing him.

—retold from *The 7 Sins of Highly Defective People* by Rick Ezell

༺ EPITAPH ༻

Here lies Walter Fielding.
He bought a house.
It killed him.

—Tom Hanks as Walter Fielding, in the movie *The Money Pit*

wasn't required. Ananias and Sapphira sold some property and turned part of the money over to the church. That was fine. It was their money. But they told the church they were handing over the *full* amount. They wanted the church to think well of them.

They had thought ahead, imagining what would happen if they told the truth. And they had decided that wouldn't work for them. But they had left God out of the picture. When we tell the truth, God does things we couldn't have foreseen. It's our job to stand with God and tell the truth. It's his job to work out the details.

Poor Ananias and Sapphira. They could've had a swimming pool.

 ## midnight tale

Mr. and Mrs. Root, a happily married older couple, were at a conference and accidentally ended up in a workshop about family problems. Mr. Root said he and his wife didn't quarrel, because he let her do whatever she wanted to do.

Man: But—but suppose what she wants to do is wrong?

Mr. Root: The supposition is absurd. Why would she want to do wrong?

Man: Well, what if she didn't know it was wrong?

Mr. Root: I wouldn't marry a girl who didn't know right from wrong.

in memory of
Ananias and Sapphira

"An untruthful person will not be left unpunished."
Proverbs 19:5, ICB

Face of an Angel

Here Lies
Stephen, the first Christian martyr

THE BODY

September 2003. A man was badly wounded in Iraq. He was an anti-American foreigner who had come into Iraq "to kill American soldiers." Now his wounds were being treated by American military medics. One night they found him crying in his bed. He was overwhelmed. He couldn't understand how people he hated so much could care for him so kindly.

The medics may not have realized it, but their actions were the exact definition of *forgiveness.* They were not holding the man's murderous attempts against him. They were treating him properly, regardless of what he'd done. That's forgiveness.

Stephen took forgiveness a step further.

cause of death
Acts 7 is Stephen's long speech in which he gave the Jewish officials an earful. He ended by blasting the officials for killing Jesus. Enraged, they dragged him out of the city and stoned him.

last words
"Lord, do not hold this sin against them"
(Acts 7:60, NIV).

STONE-COLD FACT
Meredith's Book of Bible Lists gives 16 accounts of stonings in the Bible. Not all of them were successful.

Stephen was one of seven deacons recently elected to help run the church. He was speaking out powerfully for the Lord. He was working miracles.

Jesus had risen from the dead, and the church was growing like crazy. The people who had killed Jesus thought they'd gotten rid of their problem. They thought they'd secured their position as religious leaders. But the excited followers of Jesus were continuing where Jesus left off—turning people away from the hypocritical leaders, leading them toward the truth. The religious leaders had to try to put an end to it.

Just as they'd done in the case of Jesus, they brought false charges against Stephen. They brought in false witnesses. The whole story is in Acts 6, 7.

Stephen knew he was in danger. Look what had happened to Jesus. But he would not be stopped. He spoke to the leaders, going clear back to the beginning and recounting the entire Jewish history. He ended by calling them murderers for killing Jesus, the

EPITAPH

Grieve not for me,
Nor let one small tear fall.
For what you can only
   dream,
I can see. And friend
'Tis worth it all, 'tis worth
   it all.

—unknown

168

very Messiah they should have welcomed.

That didn't go over too well.

They attacked Stephen and began stoning him. While he was dying he prayed, as Jesus had prayed, for the Father to forgive them. Wow.

It's one thing for medics to "forgive" a man who no longer has any power over them. It's another to forgive the very people who are in the process of killing you. We're not promised that believers will have easy lives or the luxury of simply dying in their sleep. Stephen's death was not pretty; but it was a good death. If we live in love and forgiveness—as Stephen and Jesus did—we also can die a good death.

life line —〰〰〰

"Jesus didn't teach us to love our enemies for their good. It is for our own good—to keep from becoming the enemy."

—Russ Ford, chaplain on death row

HEART-STOPPER

It has been said: We are most like beasts when we kill; we are most like man when we judge; we are most like God when we forgive.

 **midnight tale**

Many people believe we become angels when we die. Cartoons and movies often portray angels as people who have died. But the Bible doesn't teach that. Only two angels are named in the Bible: Gabriel seems to be a special messenger (Daniel 8, 9; Luke 1), and Michael is the archangel (Daniel 10, 12; Jude 9; Revelation 12). Seraphs with six wings are mentioned in Isaiah 6. The wildest angels are the cherubs in Ezekiel 1 and 10—with four faces, eyes all around and "wheels" that move with them! Some teachers believe there are many different ranks of angels, military style. Other teachers believe that all the angels are polymorphs who can appear as any type of angel. One thing is certain: angels are not to be worshiped (Revelation 22:8, 9).

in memory of
Stephen

When he spoke of the Lord, "his face was like the face of an angel."
Acts 6:15, NIV

DEARLY DEPARTED

Here Lies
Dorcas, also called Tabitha, resident of Joppa

THE BODY

I do *not* understand some of our funeral customs.

Let's say I've been in bed with the flu for three days. I'm pale, I haven't eaten, I've lost weight—I'm not up to seeing anybody. If someone comes to the house, my family will answer the door. But they won't send anyone in to see me. "I'm sorry," they'll say, "she's pale, she hasn't eaten, she's lost weight—she's not up to seeing anybody."

But if I die and people come to the funeral home, my family will say, "She's pale, she hasn't eaten, she's lost weight . . . come on in and see her!"

cause of death
First time—illness. But the apostle Peter raised her from the dead (Acts 9). Second time—Unknown.

last words
No recorded words at all. Dorcas's life is a great example of the old proverb, "Actions speak louder than words."

life line
"I knew what my job was; it was to go out and meet the people and love them."
—Diana, Princess of Wales

Please! I'm not up to seeing anybody. I look worse than I've ever looked. I'm dead.

And what about the words we use to describe the body? The body is in an open casket at the far room in the funeral home. People come to comfort the family. Then they want to see the person. They want to be near the body. But they hesitate to say "the body."

"Where . . . uh . . . is she?" they ask. Or "Where is the deceased?" "Where is the dearly departed?" "Where are the remains?" *The remains.* Sometimes they can't say it at all. They just point: "Is the . . . uh (point) . . . in there?"

I guess people just do the best they can to cope with the loss of a loved one. It's hard to let go. Being near the body, touching it . . . is a way of hanging on a little longer.

That's what the friends of Dorcas did (Acts 9:36-43).

They had washed her body and laid it out. They were staying close by.

Then they heard the apostle Peter was in the area and sent for him. All the apostles were working miracles. Perhaps Peter could bring their beloved Dorcas back.

When Peter arrived, he could tell immediately how loved Dorcas was. The friends were not only crying, they were clutching clothing that she had made for them. Her life had been a life of caring and giving, a life of service.

If we love someone who dies, we want to keep something of theirs: photos, clothing, jewelry, a lock of hair. And we treasure dearly anything they've given us. At funeral homes, you will see family and friends stroking the sweater they're wearing: "He gave me this on my birthday, you know." Or they'll handle a necklace: "I remember what she said when she gave this to me."

I hope people feel that way about me when they're looking at my . . . uh . . . remains.

of grave concern

Time is now fleeting, the
   moments are passing,
Passing from you and from
   me;
Shadows are gathering,
   death-beds are coming,
Coming for you and for
   me.
   —third verse of the hymn
   "Softly and Tenderly Jesus
   Is Calling" by Will
   Lamartine Thompson
   (died 1909)

DEATH
SENTENCE
This troubled world is
   sighing now,
The flu is at the door;
And many folks are dying
   now
Who never died before.
                    —unknown

STONE-COLD FACT
The national
Generosity Index listed the residents of
Mississippi as the
most generous people
in the nation in 2003.

Project Linus is a 100 percent volunteer, non-profit organization. Members make blankets to donate to traumatized or seriously ill children. By the end of the second quarter of 2003 more than 730,000 kids in need of a hug had received these security blankets.

in memory of
Dorcas

She always did good and helped the poor.
Acts 9:36

✝ DEAD MEAT

Here Lies
Herod Agrippa I, king of Judea

THE BODY
Cyrus Teed.

He said he'd received "divine illumination."

He started a new religion and moved to Florida to build a new Jerusalem.

He said he was the Messiah. And his followers believed him. When he died in 1908, they kept his body. Teed had promised to rise from the dead and take them all to Heaven.

So they waited. And waited . . .

Then Teed's body began to rot. The health officials stepped in and demanded that the body be buried. And that was the end of that. Ha! Some messiah.

cause of death
"An angel of the Lord struck him down, and he was eaten by worms and died" (Acts 12:23, NIV).

last words
His last words were spoken moments before he died, but the Bible doesn't tell us what he said. It merely states that he "delivered a public address to the people." The last words recorded at that time were the words of the people shouting back at him: "This is the voice of a god, not of a man" (Acts 12:22, NIV).

New religions and new "messiahs" spring up all the time. It's been happening for centuries. People enjoy feeling powerful. People enjoy having followers.

King Herod Agrippa I was already powerful. He already had followers, fans. He was also a wicked king whom many people would probably have liked to see dead. But God allowed his reign to continue.

Then one day King Herod Agrippa I stepped over the line.

The first part of Acts 12 tells us something of Herod Agrippa I. He had killed the apostle James. Then he saw how much that pleased the Jewish leaders (the same leaders who had killed Jesus and Stephen). So he ordered the apostle Peter put in prison. King Herod Agrippa I was struttin' his stuff.

Later he moved to the coast. (A little palace by the sea?) He threatened and scared those residents. On the day he died, he was making a royal appearance, wearing his royal robes. I guess the people decided to kiss up to him—after all, he did control their food supply. So they began to shout that he was a god.

That's when King Herod Agrippa I passed the point of no return. He accepted their praise, the kind of praise that should go only to the real God.

EPITAPH

Here lies the body of W. W.
Who never more will
trouble you, trouble you.
—unknown

Boom. Struck down and eaten by worms. Some god.

There is only one God—God the Father, Son and Spirit. The next time you hear about a new religion, look at the leader. Does he teach the truths of the Bible? Does he point his followers to himself or to the true God?

If he doesn't, get out of there fast. The worms are coming.

HEART-STOPPER

Little girl: I like to jump on my pogo stick and bounce right up to Heaven.
Art Linkletter: What do you see up there?
Girl: Girl angels, dog angels, cat angels and fish angels.
Art: No *boy* angels?
Girl: No, boy angels and worm angels don't go to Heaven.

—from the book *Kids Say the Darndest Things*

midnight tale

The Herods were the kings of Judea during the New Testament era. All the Herods were horrible. Herod the Great was the king who ordered all the baby boys killed when Jesus was born. He also killed his favorite wife, three sons and others. His son Herod Antipas is the one who had John the Baptist killed. One of Herod the Great's sons, whom he had killed, was the father of Herod Agrippa I, today's subject.

in memory of
Herod Agrippa I

"You said in your heart, . . . 'I will make myself like the Most High.' But you are brought down to the grave."
Isaiah 14:13-15, niv

SHE DYED AND THEN SHE DIED

Here Lies
Lydia, a businesswoman

THE BODY

You wouldn't think of hospitality as a scary subject, but listen to this: "Don't forget to show hospitality to strangers, for some who have done this have entertained angels without realizing it!" (Hebrews 13:2, NLT).

The writer is referring back to a story of Abraham in Genesis 18, 19. The first verse says the Lord appeared to Abraham. Then it says there were three visitors. The account goes back and forth, referring to "he" and "they." Abraham served a meal. During this visit came the announcement that Abraham and Sarah would have a son in their old age.

cause of death
Unknown.

last words
The only recorded words of Lydia are in Acts 16:15, spoken to the apostle Paul and his associates right after they baptized her: "If you consider me a believer in the Lord, come and stay at my house" (NIV).

life line —⋀⋀⋀⋀⋀—
"Charm is deceptive, and beauty does not last; but a woman who fears the Lord will be greatly praised. Reward her for all she has done. Let her deeds publicly declare her praise."

Proverbs 31:30, 31, NLT

Genesis 18:33 and 19:1 say that the Lord left and the two angels went on to destroy the cities of Sodom and Gomorrah.

So who were they? Three angels? The Father, Son and Spirit? Or perhaps an Old Testament appearance of Jesus, accompanied by two angels. Freaky.

Lydia's brief appearance in Acts 16 teaches us something about hospitality.

It's interesting that these few verses (11-15) bother to tell us her occupation. She was a seller of purple cloth. Purple was a royal color, so this may have been high-class stuff. If Lydia lived today she might be the person who designs suits for the First Lady or gowns for the Academy Awards. The mere mention of her occupation indicates that she was a busy and successful person.

On this day she took time out to listen to Paul's teaching about the Lord. Then she and her household were baptized and invited Paul's group back to her house. It says she *persuaded* them to come to her house. Perhaps they hesitated to go because they felt they would be a burden to this businesswoman. Possibly she was wealthy, and Paul's group may have feared feeling a little out of place.

At any rate, this busy lady opened her home to strangers.

Jesus relied on hospitality. He didn't own a home. Luke 9:58 says, "The Son of Man has no place to rest his head" (ICB). In Paul's letters, we are encouraged to show hospitality.

It's not about having your friends and family over. It's bigger than that. It's about opening your home and sharing what you have with people you don't know, people who can't pay you back—people like visiting missionaries, a family whose house has burned, a foreign college student who can't go home for the holidays . . .

You might be entertaining an angel without realizing it.

midnight tale

These days people tend to put their guests in hotels instead of inviting them into their homes. The oldest hotel in the world is the Hoshi Ryokan in Awazu, Japan. It was first an inn built in A.D. 717 near a spring that people thought had miraculous healing powers. The hotel has been expanded to have many rooms. People still go there to enjoy bathing in the therapeutic spring waters.

in memory of
Lydia

"She invited us in her home."
Acts 16:15, NIV

✝ Talked to Death

Here Lies
Eutychus, a young man of Troas

THE BODY

I can understand why some young people don't want to go to church. Ministers can be boring and long-winded. And they sometimes say the strangest things:

"If you're here this morning . . ." *Of course I'm here.*

"We'd like to pray for those who are sick within their bodies." *Have you ever been sick without your body?*

"Turn over in your Bible to the book of Ecclesiastes." *It's gonna be tough for Mrs. Wigglesworth to get in her Bible, much less turn over.*

I don't think the apostle Paul was a boring preacher. And I don't think he said strange things. He wrote all the books of the New Testament from Romans to Philemon, and probably Hebrews. His writing indicates that he would have been a forceful, interesting speaker.

cause of death
First time—He fell from the third floor window while the apostle Paul was preaching a long sermon (Acts 20:7-12). Second time—Unknown.

last words
No recorded words.

STONE-COLD FACT
Several different studies have found that people who attend church live longer.

But Acts 20 tells us that he could be long-winded.

I think this is one of the funniest accounts in the Bible, even though a young man named Eutychus died.

I like Eutychus. It was midnight and he was in church (probably meeting in a house). He could have been out eating some fish tacos with his friends or home watching a movie. But he came to learn about God. The apostle Paul was scheduled to leave the next day, but he had so much to tell the people. So he was preaching on and on. No matter how interesting the sermon is, a kid can only take so much. Eutychus's mistake was sitting in the window. He dropped off . . . and dropped out!

Eutychus died from the fall. Of course it was horrible, and I'm sorry to be laughing, but what a picture!

The apostle Paul raised Eutychus back to life. I suppose this shocking event jolted everybody awake because they went back inside and Paul talked on until dawn! It seems Eutychus also went back in and stayed till the end! He probably sat

EPITAPH

There was a young fellow
named Hall
Who fell in the spring in
the fall.
'Twould have been a sad
thing
If he had died in the
spring;
But he didn't—he died in
the fall.

—unknown

near the front this time.

Go to church. Get involved in a youth group, a small group, Fellowship of Christian Athletes or a Bible club at your school. Find people there who can teach you more about God and help you stay close to him. The church—all believers all over the world—is the family God is putting together to live with him in Heaven.

Go to church. But steer clear of the windows.

HEART-STOPPER

When the famous Anglican preacher John Wesley (died 1791) was forbidden to preach in a certain church, instead of giving up, he went to a nearby cemetery where his father was buried, and using his father's tomb as a pulpit, he preached the gospel of Christ.

Another famous evangelist, George Whitefield, the "lightning rod of the Great Awakening" (died 1770), returned from a preaching tour one night, extremely tired. As he lit a candle and prepared to climb the stairs to his bedroom, he noticed a group of people gathered in front of his house. So he invited them into his foyer and, candle in hand, preached his last message from the stairway. That night he died in his sleep. What a way to go!

midnight tale

A sleep researcher at Cornell University said that high school and college students are walking zombies because they don't get enough sleep. His study showed that only one percent of students are fully awake all day long.

in memory of
Eutychus

"I was glad when they said to me, 'Let us go to the house of the LORD.'"
Psalm 122:1, NLT

CSI

Here Lies
Thomas, one of Jesus' 12 apostles

THE BODY

Mary Baker Eddy founded the Christian Science religion. After teaching that there was no such thing as sickness and death, she got sick and died. It always has amazed me that her followers continued to hold on to her teachings anyway!

I'm a suspicious person. I would have needed some more evidence.

That's why I've always felt that Thomas got a bad rap. Our youth group sang a song with the line, "Don't be a doubting Thomas." *Why not?* I thought. *Why should he believe until he had proof?*

Some of the greatest voices in Christianity started out as skeptics. Doubting Thomases. They went after the evidence, intending to prove that Christianity was false.

cause of death

Thomas's death is not recorded in the Bible. Tradition says that Thomas traveled to foreign places, preaching, and that he was martyred.

last words

His last recorded words were spoken to Jesus when Thomas was convinced Jesus had risen from the dead: "My Lord and my God!" (John 20:28, NIV).

But they found—to their surprise—that the evidence, in fact, supported Christianity. The Bible *was* true. Jesus Christ *did* rise from the dead. Their messages now carry more weight because they demanded proof. They became well-known because of their quest for truth.

There was Lew Wallace who later wrote the classic *Ben-Hur.*

C.S. Lewis wrote the incomparable *Mere Christianity* (and other books) as well as the wonderful *Chronicles of Narnia* series. At one point, C.S. Lewis "maintained that God did not exist. He was very angry with God for not existing" (Kathryn Lindskoog).

Josh McDowell said that the only thing he'd ever gotten out of religion was the money he took out of the offering plate to buy a milk shake! But after tireless investigation, he wrote the compelling little book *More Than a Carpenter* and the detailed, scholarly *Evidence That Demands a Verdict.*

And there was Lee Strobel. Same story, same results. His book *The Case for Christ* has flown off bookstore shelves across the country.

I love it that Thomas didn't believe Jesus had been raised from the dead. You just don't accept something like that on the word of a few excited women or some men who are half crazy with grief.

John 20:24-31 portrays the scene. Thomas was suspicious. He made his position clear: "I will not believe until I touch the nail marks in his hands and the mark of the spear in his side." Period.

Thomas lived with his doubts for one week. Then Jesus showed up to offer proof positive. "Examine the evidence, Thomas. Touch these nail marks. Touch my side."

The results of Thomas's investigation are in the files. So are the results of Lew, C.S., Josh and Lee. You can examine their findings. And you can conduct your own investigation. The evidence is all there.

Case closed.

of grave concern

"I will not believe unless I see the bodies myself."

—an Iraqi man who was being interviewed regarding the deaths of Uday and Qusay Hussein.

life line —/\/\/\/\/\

"How can I be evidence of what's invisible to me? But when I am reflecting you I see more clearly."

—from the song "Though the Earth Give Way" by Andrea Summer

EPITAPH

Stranger, stop and cast an eye,
As you are now, so once was I.
As I am now, so you shall be—
Prepare for death and follow me.

—colonial verse, variations of which are seen on numerous old tombstones

HEART-STOPPER

In 1858 a man named William Herschel claimed that no two fingerprints are the same and that they don't change with a person's age. Sir Francis Galton (1822-1911) was the scientist who made advances in identifying various fingerprint patterns. But long before these men lived, Chinese potters signed their work with their fingerprints. Had they already figured out the uniqueness of fingerprints?

 ## midnight tale

At the Tomb of the Unknown Soldier in Arlington, Virginia, there are actually the bodies of several soldiers, representing different wars. In 1998, the body of the Vietnam War soldier was exhumed. Thanks to new technology in DNA evidence, the body was identified.

in memory of
Thomas

"By believing in [Jesus] you will have life."
John 20:31, NLT

Never Too Late

Here Lies
James, the half-brother of Jesus

THE BODY

America's Most Wanted did the story. Police caught up with, and finally arrested, a high school girl. She wasn't who she said she was. And she wasn't a high school girl. She was a young woman in her early 30s. She had been moving around all over the country, changing her name, posing as a teenager and attending different high schools.

Authorities pieced together her history and discovered she'd had an absolutely horrific childhood. They believe that, in some twisted way, she was trying to reclaim the lost days of her youth by reliving her school years over and over.

James might have liked to live his life over too—but his problem was not from a bad childhood. James's problem was himself.

cause of death

Tradition says he was martyred around A.D. 62.

last words

The last words he wrote in the book of James are: "Remember this: Whoever turns a sinner from the error of his way will save him from death and cover over a multitude of sins" (James 5:20, NIV).

EPITAPH

Thro' a long life in devious
   paths I trod
And liv'd alas! forgetful of
   my God;
But oh! The triumph of
   redeeming Power
A Sinner ransomed at the
   Eleventh hour.

—from the epitaph of
Elezer Holmes, in
Plymouth, Massachusetts,
died 1798 at age 84

James was the half-brother of Jesus. Matthew 13:55, 56 tells us that Mary and Joseph had other children. According to John 7:5, none of the siblings believed Jesus was who he said he was.

But Jesus' resurrection changed all that. In Acts 1:14 we find Jesus' brothers praying with the apostles. If James hadn't become a full-fledged believer by then, at least he was a seeker.

First Corinthians 15 lists people to whom Jesus appeared after his resurrection. Most teachers think the James in verse 7 is his brother James. By the time of Galatians 2 he was a prominent leader in the church of Jerusalem. James the apostle had already died.

This James wrote the book of James. And in it I think you can see how he is trying to make up for lost time. He writes passionately about getting busy for God. He says strong things about controlling our words. I imagine he had said hateful things to Jesus in the early days. Words he wished he could take back.

of grave concern

We make jokes about reincarnation.

Dilbert: *What if I come back as a cow?*

Dogbert: *You'll save a fortune in milk.*

. . . .

Frank: *Do you think you've had previous lives?*

Ernest: *I hope so. I'd hate to think I got this far behind in just one lifetime!*

Some people really believe in reincarnation, but the Bible does not teach reincarnation. We have one life, then eternity.

James made up for the time he'd wasted. So remember that if there are some things you've said or done that you'd like to take back. It's never too late.

The young woman from *America's Most Wanted* can recover from her damaged childhood if she finds God. It's never too late.

But the sooner the better.

SIX-FEET-DEEP THOUGHT

Actor Denzel Washington said, "Acting is just a way of making a living, the family is life." James's family certainly was his life, because Jesus was a part of his family. James just didn't catch on for a while.

HEART-STOPPER

Through this toilsome
    world, alas!
Once and only once I pass;
If a kindness I may show,
If a good deed I may do
To a suffering fellow man,
Let me do it while I can.
No delay, for it is plain
I shall not pass this way
    again.

—unknown

in memory of
James

"James, a servant of God and of the Lord Jesus Christ."
James 1:1, ICB

✝ Life Sentence

Here Lies
Paul, the apostle—formerly Saul of Tarsus

THE BODY

Brace yourself.

Remember reading about the zombies—the Pharisees? Remember how horrible they were and how Jesus verbally tore into them? Remember they were the ones who plotted to take Jesus' life, killed Stephen, egged on King Herod Agrippa I to kill other key Christian leaders? Well, the apostle Paul was one of those Pharisees.

That's right. He was Saul of Tarsus, a Pharisee. He stood by and watched Stephen be killed. He was out to track down Christians. He was very passionate about his purpose. The thing is, he probably truly thought he was honoring God. He must have considered Jesus to be a

cause of death

After his fourth missionary journey Paul was put in prison in Rome. He was probably beheaded in A.D. 67 or 68, about 30 years after he first met Jesus.

last words

"The time of my death is near. I have fought a good fight, I have finished the race, and I have remained faithful. And now the prize awaits me—the crown of righteousness that the Lord, the righteous Judge, will give me" (2 Timothy 4:7, 8, NLT).

false prophet who had led people away from the truth. So Saul of Tarsus was going to do something about it. (He later said God showed him mercy because he was acting in ignorance. See 1 Timothy 1:13.)

He was so fiery, who knows how many Christian deaths he would have been responsible for if the Lord hadn't stopped him? But the Lord did stop him.

Dead in his tracks.

The resurrected Jesus powerfully confronted Saul right in the middle of one of his murderous trips (Acts 9). Jesus told Saul he was way off base and sent him to meet with a Christian man who would help put him on the right path. Not surprisingly, the Christian man wasn't too thrilled. He thought the Lord had the wrong guy. "Uh, Lord . . . surely you don't mean Saul . . . he's the one trying to kill us."

It took the apostle Paul a little while to regroup from his complete turnaround. Then he applied his same original passion to telling the world about the Lord. At first, the church was suspicious of him. "Isn't he the man who raised havoc in Jerusalem?" they asked (Acts 9:21, NIV). But his conversion was for real. Paul dedicated the remainder of his life to spreading the word.

Almost immediately, he found himself on the receiving end of the attacks against Christians. The very group of leaders he was once a part of conspired to kill him (Acts 9:23). It was a roller-coaster ride from there on out. The rest of the book of Acts outlines all Paul's adventures. He traveled far and wide, starting churches and training ministers. What he survived in the process is unbelievable: beatings, stoning, threats, shipwreck, health problems, imprisonment . . . read the list in 2 Corinthians 11:23-33.

of grave concern

In Paul's day people were out to destroy the church and anyone who believed in Jesus. So Christians began to have meetings in secret, in fear for their lives. Sometimes they met in catacombs, which were underground cave tunnels. Tradition says that the friends of Paul buried him in such a place. These tunnels served as both graves for dead Christians and refuges for living ones.

life line —∧∧∧∧∧∧

"Friends don't let friends go to Hell."

—seen on a T-shirt

HEART-STOPPER

"Many of us believe that, at its core, being a Christian means living a good life. But perhaps, at its core, being a Christian means living a dangerous life."
—Vince Antonucci, lead pastor of ForeFront Church in Virginia Beach, Virginia

Anybody looking for a little risk and adventure should read about the life of Paul. If you think Christianity is boring, you must not be doing it right.

 ### midnight tale

Mike Yaconelli, cofounder of Youth Specialties, whom some call the "father of modern-day youth ministry," was speaking at the 2003 National Youth Workers Convention in Charlotte, North Carolina. He said this: "If I were to have a heart attack right at this moment, I hope I would have just enough air in my lungs and just enough strength in me to utter one last sentence as I fell to the floor: 'What a ride!'" Just three days later, on October 30, 2003, Mike died in a tragic car accident. Like Mike, the apostle Paul certainly could have exclaimed: "What a ride!"

in memory of
Paul

*"The Lord stood with me and gave me strength,
that I might preach the Good News."*
2 Timothy 4:17, NLT

Rest in Peace

Here Lies
John the apostle, Jesus' best friend

THE BODY

I didn't get it. *The Matrix.* I had to keep giving up and simply enjoy the stunts and the special effects. If I ever watch *The Matrix* again, I'm sitting next to the apostle John. He's the only person I can think of who would really understand it.

The best I could tell . . . there were two different worlds going on in *The Matrix.* If the characters caught on, they could become part of the other world, the real and better one. But the bad guys didn't want that to happen. They wanted to keep people back in the first world, where they had more control. It seemed to be about being brave enough to move into the second world.

cause of death

John was banished to the island of Patmos, where he saw the vision he wrote down as the book of Revelation. After his release and return to Ephesus, tradition says he died of natural causes—the only one of the apostles not to be martyred.

last words

John's last recorded words are also the last words in the Bible. "Come, Lord Jesus. The grace of the Lord Jesus be with God's people. Amen" (Revelation 22:20, 21, NIV).

199

Like I said, the apostle John could have explained it perfectly.

The apostle John was Jesus' best friend. He referred to himself as the one Jesus loved. Though none of the apostles clearly understood what Jesus was trying to do, John came the closest. He wrote five books:

The Gospel of John—Like Matthew, Mark and Luke it is an account of Jesus' life. But it's different than the other three because John understood more of what was going on. Matthew, Mark and Luke tell many events from Jesus' life and they quote from his sermons. John tells some of those things too. And he explains them to us. Throughout the book, John keeps whispering to the readers: "He said this because . . ." and "What he meant was . . ." But the bonus part of John's Gospel is an emphasis—over and over—that Jesus is God.

First John, 2 John and 3 John—These are three tiny letters John wrote. First John is all about love. Pretty amazing from a guy who once wanted to call down fire from Heaven to consume a whole village (Luke 9:54).

Revelation—Revelation is the vision John saw about the end of the world. Like *The Matrix,* it is filled with stunts and special effects. You're never quite sure if the events being described are taking place in the first world of Earth or in the second world of Heaven and Hell. Watching the Revelation unfold was hard on John. He fell down, terrified (Revelation 1:17), he cried (5:4), he was astonished (17:6). Same effect *The Matrix* had on me!

We are unraveling a mystery here. John was Jesus' best friend, so we need to pay attention to him. This is inside information. John understood the two worlds. And he clued us in by what he wrote in his books.

What did John tell us? He told us that Jesus is God. He told us that it's all about love. And he told us that wild things will happen at the end of time—and there *is* a Heaven and Hell.

Get it?

SIX-FEET-DEEP THOUGHT

"We feel young when we focus . . . on the eternal. . . . [We] are spiritual beings having a short stint in a physical experience."

—Joni Eareckson Tada, who has been in a wheelchair since 1967

life line —〰〰〰

"A friend is somebody you want to be around when you feel like being by yourself."

—Barbara Burrow

HEART-STOPPER

John 21:20 says that, at the Last Supper, John leaned back against Jesus. Someone described that scene by saying that John heard the heartbeat of God.

midnight tale

In July 2003, VH-1 and *People* magazine selected the 200 greatest pop culture icons of all time. The Top 10, counting from number 10 up to number 1 were: 10. Michael Jackson. 9. Princess Diana. 8. Michael Jordan. 7. Madonna. 6. Marilyn Monroe. 5. Tom Cruise. 4. Lucille Ball. 3. Elvis Presley. 2. Superman. 1. Oprah Winfrey. When Peter Castro of *People* magazine was asked why these pop culture icons are important, he said: "Who else are we gonna look up to?"

Who else? Well, I have some suggestions. And the apostle John wouldn't be a bad place to start.

in memory of
John the apostle

"There is a friend who sticks closer than a brother."
Proverbs 18:24, NIV

✝ Ìt Ìs Fìnìshed

Here ~~Lies~~ Lives
Jesus of Nazareth, Son of God

†HE BODY

Everybody wants a piece of the cross.

One of those travel guys on TV visited a museum in Europe that was filled with religious relics. There was a tooth supposedly from John the Baptist, a piece of the tablecloth claimed to be from the Last Supper and a piece of wood allegedly taken from the actual cross of Jesus. Local people told the travel guy that there are places all around the world displaying pieces of the "actual cross" and that, if all those pieces were gathered together, about 40 crosses could be constructed from them!

Everybody wants a piece of the cross.

Cemeteries are full of crosses of many styles. There's a Presbyterian cross design, a Russian Orthodox cross design, an Episcopal cross design . . . and simple generic

cause of death
Crucifixion . . . or love—depending on how you look at it.

last words
"It is finished" (John 19:30, NIV).

~~ **EPITAPH** ~~
He is not here.

WORDS TO LIVE BY

"Neither death nor life, neither angels nor demons, neither the present nor the future, nor any powers, neither height nor depth, nor anything else in all creation, will be able to separate us from the love of God that is in Christ Jesus our Lord."

Romans 8:38, 39, NIV

crosses. They decorate the graves of believers and nonbelievers, grandfathers and babies, police officers and criminals, soldiers and civilians.

life line —〰〰〰

Love so amazing, so divine, Demands my soul, my life, my all.

—last line of the hymn "When I Survey the Wondrous Cross" by Isaac Watts (died 1748)

Everybody wants a piece of the cross.

The Nazis of Germany marched under the swastika symbol, a broken cross. The flower children of the 1960s popularized the peace symbol, an upside-down cross. There's a Celtic cross on the cover of this book. Celtic crosses often have ornate designs. The Christian ones may have designs representing specific Bible stories, characters or other Christian symbols. Others contain designs with no apparent meaning. Still others include occultic or pagan symbols. The Celtic cross is seen on Christian books as well as on New Age books

HEART-STOPPER

Almost 800 years before the cross, Isaiah predicted that the Lord would "swallow up death forever" (25:8, NIV).

and in openly pagan literature.

Everybody wants a piece of the cross.

Crosses are worn by priests, soccer moms, bikers, preps, heavy metal rockers, executives and vampire slayers. Crosses are displayed on buildings, carried in pockets, enclosed in coffins, dangled from car mirrors.

People change the design of the cross, break it, turn it upside down, wear it and bury it. But they can't seem to leave it alone.

Everybody wants a piece of the cross.

Because deep inside everybody knows that the cross represents power. The mistake of some people is thinking the power is in the

DEATH
SENTENCE

There are Seven Sayings of the Cross, seven last words Jesus spoke as he was dying. They can be found in Matthew 27:46; Luke 23:34-46; John 19:26-30. They are filled with love and compassion . . . but also with desperation and need. Very much God. Very much man.

object. But the power is not in the wood or the silver or the gold, not in the shape or the angles. The power is—and always was—in Jesus himself. He is the strongest power there is. He's the power of creation. He's the power that chose to save us—and the only power that could. He is the light that overpowers darkness. He is the love that overpowers fear and hate. He is the life that overpowers death.

Take your piece of the cross. But hold on to the power behind it.

 midnight tale

Actor Bruce Marchiano starred as Jesus in *Matthew*, a word-for-word video portrayal of the Gospel. During the filming of the crucifixion scene, an actor playing a Roman soldier grabbed Bruce's wrist to "nail" it to the cross. Bruce said, "I can't describe the panic that went through my heart when I saw that nail." Later Bruce wrote in his journal: "I believe every Christian should hang on a cross for at least thirty seconds. Their lives will never be the same." (*Christian Reader*, Mar-Apr/'96)

in memory of
Jesus

"Do not be afraid. I am the First and the Last. I am the Living One; I was dead, and behold I am alive for ever and ever! And I hold the keys of death."
Revelation 1:17, 18, NIV

Topical Index